FISHING CONNECTICUT WATERS

Reprints from The Fisherman

by
Tim Coleman

MT PUBLICATIONS
MYSTIC, CONNECTICUT

Library of Congress Cataloging-in-Publication Data

Coleman, Tim, 1946-
    Fishing Connecticut waters.

    Includes index.
    1. Fishing — Connecticut.   I. Title.
QL628.C8C65   1988   799.1'66146   88-26722

ISBN 0-929775-00-7

First printing — 1983
Revised and expanded — 1988

MT PUBLICATIONS
Two Denison Avenue
Mystic, CT 06355

About This Book

In the January 30, 1983 issue of *The Fisherman* we ran an offer for reprints from back issues. It only ran once but we received more letters from it than anything we'd put in print in awhile. We received so many letters that we decided the thing to do was make up a book from past articles. The first one was "Fishing Connecticut Waters" which was followed by four other titles. The first printing of Connecticut Waters is sold out so we now feel it's time to bring out a newer, expanded version of the book which started the series five years ago.

While this book is obviously aimed at our Connecticut readers, it isn't limited to that state's waters exclusively. For instance the first chapter deals with fluke fishing across the Sound in New York. While obviously not in Connecticut, this area and others are of definite interest to people in the state.

A lot of time and effort went into tracking down the info brought together here. If we do say so, it would take the average person, without connections, quite a few years to learn what's printed here. We do hope you enjoy it, and at this time would like to thank the best people in the world: the readers of *The Fisherman,* whose support made our growth and prosperity possible the last ten years. While we are giving thanks, we should give a nod of the hat to the following anglers whose knowledge helped greatly. They are Phil Wetmore, Walt from Outdoor Sports Shop, "Patrick," Peter Fisher, Kerry Douton, Dottie Streeter, John Baldino, Luciano Bellastrini, Bob Mahoney, Silent George, Frank Hutchins, Capt. Bill Huntley, Charley Soares and the fellow I met one dark night on the Poquetanuck Cove RR bridge.

Additional people and organizations we'd like to thank are Capt. Frank Blount, Ed from Rudy's Tackle Barn, Dave Motherway, the Ct. State DEP, Stan Schwartz the diver, Mark Friese from National Ocean Service, Pat Charillo, Ted Keatley and *The Fisherman* magazine's anonymous source for wreck information.

Contents

Contents

CHAPTER 1

Orient Shoal – Gardiner's Island Fluke

A boat coming out an eastern Connecticut port has a lot of options for fluke fishing. Napatree Point can be good at times and the waters off Misquamicut and Isabella Beach often hold the biggest fluke of the season. Other boats from Niantic to Westbrook often head for a couple other locations: Orient Shoal and Gardiner's Island.

Over the last couple seasons, these spots were continually mentioned in our Fishing Reports section. Even on slow weeks, these areas—especially Gardiner's Island—always had a few fish around. With that in mind, it seemed a good idea to do a story on them.

Around Gardiner's Island there are a lot of nooks and crannies holding fluke. We'll take a look at just one of them here. The spot near the island we are going to talk about is on the east side. If you look on a chart you should see Eastern Plain Point. It lies to the north of Tobaccolot Bay. If you run your finger out along the Point, you see a finger of blue shoal water with a couple high spots at the tip of the shoal. On the incoming tide, a rip line sets up here on an east to west line.

This rip and the water around it provide plenty of fluke. The technique on some days is the same as bluefishing. Run up ahead of the rip, drop in your rig, then drift back to the rip. If you catch a fish or two in the same spot the first couple drifts, throw a marker buoy over. Next pass, shorten your drift to cover only that water. Once you've gone past that stretch, go back right away. Don't waste time with water you haven't tested. If you make more drifts in the first area without any hits, then move down behind the rip, but not before.

Our last trip over there we noticed many, many boats drifting way back from the rip. Most of the fish taken that morning came from either the rip line or a couple hundred feet ahead. I got the distinct feeling a lot of these other boats spent too much time in relatively fishless water.

On that trip bucktails laced with squid strips took some fish, but pieces of fluke belly on the standard two-hook rig worked better. The fluke belly also took slightly bigger fish on the average than a squid strip fished on a bait rig. Four ounces was plenty to hold bottom.

Porgies frequent the east side of Gardiner's. If you get a rat-tat-tat on the squid, it's probaby a scup. The day we fished here schools of small blues popped up on slack water, but they moved way too fast for us to chase them. Besides, we wanted fluke and there was no sense going off on a tangent.

Next spot on our list is Orient Shoal. This lies off the north shore of Long Island near the town of East Marion. Look on the chart for Rocky and Terry Points. In between them is Truman Beach. Just offshore from that is the C3 can. Check out the shoal water that lies to the southwest of the can. That's Orient Shoal. On an incoming tide, a noticeable rip sets up as water flows from twenty feet up to around seven in some spots on the shoal. Like the rip off Eastern Plain Point, fluke lay anywhere from down tide of the shoal to right on the peak to up tide from it. How far up tide is anybody's guess. Once you find them, though, don't waste time in other areas.

If you get over there on slack water, you might try fishing bucktails with small squid strips on light tackle. A good place to look is the area on the accompanying chart marked with an X in a circle. We took fish here on the bucktails at a pretty good clip until the tide started. Action shut down there then and picked up over by the shoal. On a running tide, the bait rigs worked better than the bucktails. On the slack water, the bucktails outfished the bait rigs three to one.

Last trip to this shoal saw the flood create big mud boils as the tide moved over the shoal. Once the tide got going, the fishing dropped off as the water got dirtier and dirtier.

Don't overlook light tackle for fluke fishing. You can take the freshwater rods you use for largemouths and have a ball with fluke in the one to two pound class. If you have small conventional tackle, you might want to invest

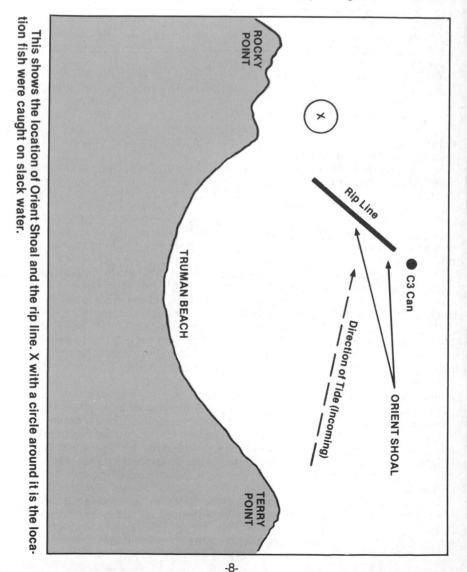

This shows the location of Orient Shoal and the rip line. X with a circle around it is the location fish were caught on slack water.

in an extension butt for a rod rated for ten to fifteen pound test line and lures from one-half to an ounce-and-a-half. These sticks are ideal for using half ounce white bucktails or small sinkers during slack water or the weaker ends of the tide. The extension butt makes it easier for holding the rod while drift fishing and gives extra leverage should a big fluke or weakfish get into the act.

Not long after our last fluke trip, I went out sharkin' with Fred Gallagher on the "Kerritim II" out of Point Judith. I watched and took pictures as a fellow named Pete caught a 110 lb. brown shark on tackle that looked familiar. Looked familiar? Yes, the same type gear that is often used on blues—or sharks—is often put to use on fluke. With such a comparative "cannon," a fluke in the two to four pound range can't give much account of himself. Put the same fish on a light, baitcasting outfit and watch the difference. Unfortunately, tides play a role in determining tackle. Whenever possible, though, give the light stuff a chance.

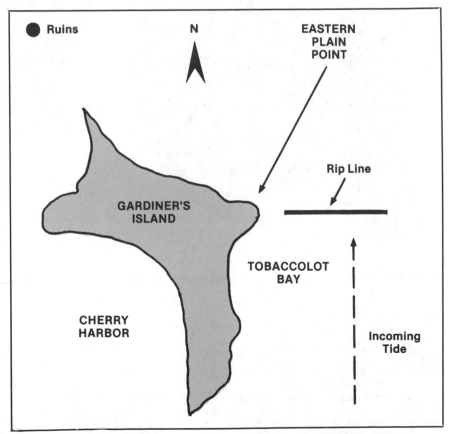

Shows the location of the rip line that set up on an incoming tide.

Blackfishing usually starts in mid-April. Sometimes the old adage about the birth of the apple blossoms coinciding with the blacks' arrival is true. The fall, however, from September on, is generally the better time for big fish in most spots.

CHAPTER 2

Blackfishing
Close to New Haven

What do Charles Island, the New Haven Harbor breakwaters and Six Mile Reef all have in common? According to a Polish fellow nicknamed the "Fishing Pole" these locations are all decent blackfishing spots.

Recently Walt Janeczek, who runs Outdoor Sports in New Haven, agreed to let me and readers in on some fishing tips. The following is the result of my conversation with Walt during a rainy Monday afternoon.

Walt got his nickname from a disc jockey at radio station WELI. The nickname came as a result of continued, good-natured jesting between the two. Now, on to some blackfishing.

Moving west to east the first spot marked on a chart for me was Charles Island, located off Milford. Water depth over the hard/rocky bottom on the western side of the island varies from ten to thirty feet. Spring is the best time and sandworms are the best bait.

Look for smaller size blacks at Charles than the other two spots we'll have a look at. Don't overlook the waters around the bell directly south of the island. Some good catches have been made there. Incoming tide is generally better for these spots off Milford.

About 3½ miles east of Charles lies the three New Haven breakwaters. The west breakwater is called Woodmont; the east jetty is known as Lighthouse. The breakwaters are good in spring and fall, with spring the best time for big fish in this particular spot.

Fellows fish these jetties in close to the rocks. Some tie their boats up to the jetties, then fish from the rocks. You want to fish the north side of the breakwaters on the incoming tide and the south sides on the drop. Green crabs are the best bait.

Last spot within easy reach of New Haven fishermen is Six Mile Reef, located about 2½ miles south of Kelsey Point. Water depth is 27 to 39 feet on the reef, dropping off to anywhere from 50 to 90 feet on the north and south edges.

The reef has traditionally been good from Thanksgiving up until the second snowstorm. If it doesn't snow much, blacks can be taken at the reef all winter long. Crabs are the best bait here and again, incoming is the best water.

Once you get used to any of these spots you have to use the right terminal gear for maximum results. You want two number three Virginia style hooks snelled on tarred line as shown in the photo. The tarred line (very hard to buy in the average bait shop) holds up well against chaffing on rocks.

Store these rust-prone hooks by sticking them in a piece of cloth soaked in olive oil. The oil retards rust. Don't use machine oil as this leaves an odor on your hooks which blacks detect.

On these hooks use green crabs for bait. Fiddler crabs, nicknamed "china backs" will get more small fish. Prepare your crabs by taking off the shell on the back first, then cutting up the crab. If you put shell and all on your hook, blacks can suck the meat out of the shell without becoming easily hooked.

Dead crabs work just as well as live ones but frozen crabs are a much softer bait than unfrozen ones, hence the meat is easier for a blackfish to steal off the hook.

Sinker weight for the crab rig is determined by your line test. You need one ounce of sinker for ever ten pound test of your line. For instance a blackfisherman using thirty pound test needs a three ounce sinker.

Blackfishing usually starts in mid-April. Sometimes the old adage about the birth of the apple blossoms coinciding with the blacks' arrival is true. The fall however, from September on, is generally the better time for big fish in most spots.

In late May to early July blackfish spawn. At times blacks hit the surface trying to use that force to push the roe out of themselves. It's during this spawning time that blackfish grab a trolled spinner and worm combo meant for bass.

Chumming with mussels and crushed clams will intensify your results. But chumming will also attract other species, some of which will be undesireable. Don't be surprised if you hook the biggest bass of your life, especially if you're chumming while anchored over a piece of bottom where sand and rocks merge. Such a junction is a good bass spot no matter where you fish.

If you get a black hooked but he won't leave his rocky condominium, bang on the butt of the rod a couple of times. If your line is taut, the banging sends unbearable vibrations down to the hooked black. He'll usually move out of his fortress to escape the unnatural vibrations.

At the end of our talk I noticed Walt's dispensing information had attracted a third party. The fellow smiled, then said, I never knew about some of that stuff about blackfish. Well, that was one satisfied "reader," and even before I approached my typewriter. How about you, did you learn anything???

Some old timers favor two Virginia hooks on a tarred line. The tarred line (hard to locate nowadays) holds up to chaffing on rocks.

CHAPTER 3

Spring Bassfishing in the Lower Connecticut River

Long about this time, I'll bet you are itchy to get a bass or two. You could run up to Matunuck or the West Wall in Rhode Island, or you could go to the Thames or maybe the upper portion of the Niantic or might just try the lower Connecticut River. The area from the East Breakwater up to Ragged Rock Creek usually has some striper action just about now.

You won't be after cows. School fish under ten pounds are what you're most likely to find taking small Rebels or RedFins.

To best follow along with the story, get chart 12375 in front of you. All the places we'll be taking a look at are on this chart. The accompanying map is a piece lifted from that particular chart. First place is near the banks of Great Island, located on the east side of the river. Right at the start of the dropping tide, you want to anchor your boat about one cast-length away from the shore. Cast the small plugs both into the shore line and to the west out onto the flats. If you like trolling, use a spinner and worm and move slowly throughout the area marked by the arrows and a straight line.

Fishing at this time of year dies at dusk so you want to be on the water after work, right up until the sun goes down. The best time would be a dropping tide in the evening. To determine the proper time to start fishing, get a tide chart. Approximately an hour and a half after high water at the mouth of the river, the current in the river will start to drop or flow to the south. For instance, if high water was at, say 4 p.m., you should be off Great Island by 5:30. The hour-and-a-half figure is an approximation. When the river is full of rainfall, or when the wind blows hard from the north, that water might start to ebb earlier.

If the river is somewhat discolored, you can still catch fish. However, if it is very high and very muddy—go home. Not only don't the fish not feed well, but your boat might take a shot from such things as telephone poles or other debris coming down river.

If you work the Great Island area without a touch, try over to the southwest to the spot marked on the chart as "Flats Area." Try drifting and casting the small plugs or bucktails in here. Also work the rock piles to the northwest and southwest of the Flats Area. Take careful note of the pile of rocks labeled on the chart as Griswold Piers. The fellow who gave the info for this article noted many a lower unit has come to an end here.

Another place to fish this month—and another place to watch for rocks—is the mouth of Ragged Rock Creek located on the west side of the river. Bear in mind, the rocks outside of the mouth of the creek show at low water, but are covered on the higher portions of the tide. As with Great Island, you want to cast small swimmers in towards the bank or work the rock piles over—carefully.

I inquired about herring in Ragged Rock Creek, but was told the place probably didn't have a run due to shallow water. However, my host said he's seen quite a few blue back herring in the lower river, and toward the end of May has snagged a few alewives. One good bet to locate the latter is to use your depth finder up river between the RR bridge and the I-95 bridge.

Now back to lure fishing. Towards the beginning of May, you start checking out Foley's Point and can #7 for some bass. On your chart, Foley's is the first unmarked point of land to the north of Lynde Point at the mouth of the river. Bucktails work well here when cast from an anchored boat. Get to this spot at the start of the dropping tide. A rip will make up between the can and point of land. Anchor your boat up current from the rip. Cast a bucktail off to the northeast, then let it swing down into the rip. As the bucktail moves down tide, it will sink. If you've got the boat positioned right, it will be down on the bottom in seven to ten feet of water at the edge of the rip. If you anchor too far up current, the bucktail will touch down up ahead of the rip. You want the lure to hit the seven to ten foot depth for best results.

As the tide increases in velocity, the can will dip out of sight. That's a signal to move. From here, go over to the Spindle located on the northeast corner of the East Breakwater at the river's mouth. A smart angler positions his boat to the north of the Spindle, then casts bucktails or small plugs into the rocks of the breakwater. If no action is forthcoming, move your boat along the north face of the breakwater, working over the rocks as you go. Pay particular attention to your casting as you reach the bend in the jetty. More than one schoolie has dined in this spot. Last, if you don't get any hits, try down by the south tip of the breakwater. However, bear in mind the southern tip is usually best at the end of the tide. Also, it was the opinion of the fisherman whose experiences you are now reading about, that the tip was not too productive until sometime in June.

Speaking of June, the rip off Foley's has some weaks in it then, along with good sized blues. Blues also show up around the Flats Area off Great Island sometime in late May-early June. If you want flounder, try fishing to the south of the Spindle. During the flatfish season, there's usually a couple boats anchored at this location.

Ramps are located on the west bank of the river right under the I-95 bridge and on the east bank of the river off Smith's Neck Road. The east ramp is located on the bank of the Back River, a tributary of the Connecticut —home of spring bass action. If you get a few fish, say a silent thank you to a bass fisherman who wishes to remain anonymous.

Arrows pointing to lines off Great Island and Ragged Rock Creek are two good areas. Other worthwhile spots are the flats, shown by a circle, and the #7 can off Foley's Point plus the section from the Spindle to south tip of the breakwater.

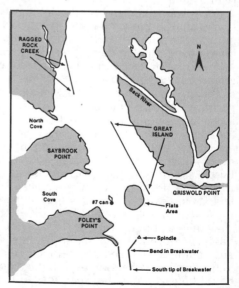

-14-

CHAPTER 4

Pawcatuck River School Bass

Would you like some info on a place you might take a small boat to cast light rigs for schoolie bass? If the answer is yes, then read on; we're about to tell you about striper fishing in the Pawcatuck River.

For those unfamiliar with eastern Connecticut, the Pawcatuck flows down between the towns of Pawcatuck and Westerly on the Connecticut-Rhode Island border. It empties into Little Narragansett Bay which, in turn, flows out into Fisher's Island Sound. On an outgoing tide, this water washes out over the Watch Hill Reefs. The reefs have long been known as a spot where anglers from several states plucked jumbo bass out from amongst the pot buoys on a variety of live baits.

With bass fishing changing to a true sport fishery rather than X pounds shipped to Fulton Market to help meet boat payments, the emphasis is now on enjoyment. The river fishing fits right into this category. Here's a place people can spend early morning or late afternoon casting a variety of small lures for the pure relaxation of the sport. Early in the year, especially on weekdays, the river isn't so crowded a person can't find a stretch off to his or her lonesome.

What you should do to follow along with the story is pick up a chart for the area. You'll be able to pinpoint spots because all names used are ones listed on the chart which was used to make the accompanying map. We might also add a tip of the hat to an unnamed source from Pawcatuck who provided a lot of the background information.

Now we'll head upriver to a point above the Westerly Yacht Club. From there we'll work our way back down, marking locations as we go. Our first stop is Stanton Weir Pt., called Whewell's Ditch by some locals because of the trench dug back into the shore.

Tackle for the river can be the same you used for the trout opener: spinning rods with 8 to 10 pound line plus small swimming plugs or tiny poppers. If you really want a blast try ultralight spinning with four pound test.

Generally people pull their small boats up to a point of land then drift with the tide, working as much water as they can. If there's a swirl under the popper or tap on the swimmer then obviously another drift is called for. Readers who have electric motors might find them ideal for pulling up quietly on feeding fish. Just remember you'll be in salty tidewater, particularly on the incoming tide. If you are not sure how your electric will react to the salt, better check your instruction booklet or dealer.

Our next stop will be on the east side of the river, this time below the Westerly Yacht Club. You'll pass through a narrow gap before coming up on the rocks which stick out of the water most of the time. Lay off a cast length or so but work the stretch carefully, all the while keeping an eye peeled for rocks that eat propellers.

Next we scoot downriver a short run to Certain Draw Point, also called Hoxie's Pt. by some locals. Try both north and south side of the point and don't be afraid to cast your lure way in tight to the undercut bank. The water is fairly deep so fish move right up into the grass on the higher tides. As

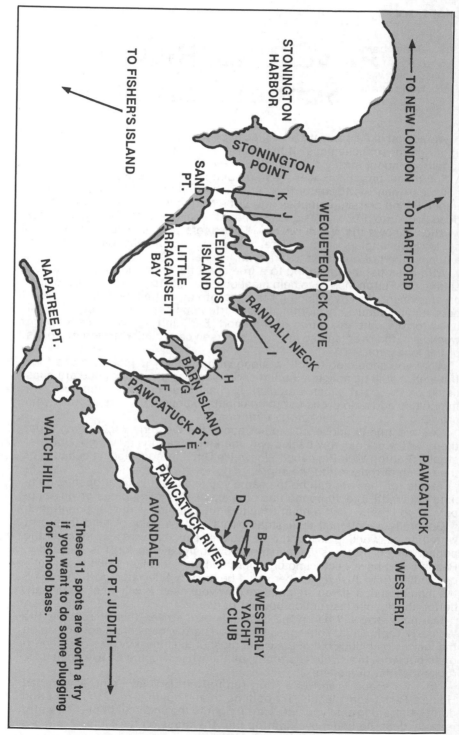

TO NEW LONDON — TO HARTFORD

STONINGTON HARBOR

STONINGTON POINT

WEQUETEQUOCK COVE

TO FISHER'S ISLAND

SANDY PT.

LEDWOODS ISLAND

LITTLE NARRAGANSETT BAY

K

J

RANDALL NECK

I

NAPATREE PT.

BARN ISLAND

H

G

F

PAWCATUCK PT.

E

WATCH HILL

PAWCATUCK RIVER

AVONDALE

D

C

B

A

WESTERLY YACHT CLUB

PAWCATUCK

WESTERLY

TO PT. JUDITH ——

These 11 spots are worth a try if you want to do some plugging for school bass.

-16-

LEGEND

A. Stanton Weir Point
B. Rocks below Westerly Yacht Club
C. Certain Draw Point
D. Docks, west side of the river
E. Halls Island
F. Seal Rocks
G. Peach Island
H. Barn Island
I. State Ramp
J. Rocks, north side of the channel
K. Sandy Point drop-off

---

always though, watch for rocks. On a couple trips last season with George Thackeray, I watched George BACK his tin boat in toward shore, peering over the motor for obstacles.

Most of the bass you'll catch in the river will be undersized so they'll have to be tossed back. That's okay, for they will be around next time you have a day off. While most bass are small, there's still a chance for something over 15 pounds, particularly further down river. Lots of the locals have stories of large fish breaking free.

Motoring down from Certain Draw Point you'll see some docks on the west side of the channel. On higher tides bass sometimes move up around the dock supports looking for a meal. Lay your casts in to shore, then work the plug back to you. The first time a schoolie whacks a surface plug cast by your son or daughter will be a lasting impression.

Hall's Island is our next landfall; it's marked E on the legend. A couple of the local sharpies who work at Harris in the town of Pawcatuck like this spot, so don't be surprised if you find a couple other boats. Most of the action will come from the channel side of the island.

If you don't get any hits at Hall's Island, take a right hand turn as you clear the mouth of the river. Your next three choices will be Seal Rocks, Perch Island and Barn Island, marked F, G and H, respectively. At Seal Rocks you drift near sunken stones tossing plugs into them. If you don't know the lay of the land, it might be advisable to tilt your motor up out of the water as you drift. Keep an eye peeled for larger fish, especially if buckies are dropping out of the river or if there's schools of flipping pogies (bunker).

At Perch Island you want to cast to the rocks on the channel side, again keeping in the back of your mind the possibility of larger fish. To the west of Perch Island we find Barn Island, not to be confused with the neck of land containing the state launch ramp. That's marked on the chart as Randall's Neck. If you ask in town, people will tell you the state ramp is at Barn Island; so be advised.

As you fish the Barn Island point, work all around it. If the wind is blowing too much for a decent drift, haul out the anchor to give the place a good going over. There's been some decent fishing here in the past.

One bonus to this whole general area is one can launch his small rig at the state ramp, then fish for bass in the early am, then try for flounder later in the day in some of the coves on the north shore of Fisher's Island or, in season, try for fluke off Napatree. If you can only fish weekends you'll have to fish early as seasonal boat traffic tends to spook fish. And, as we head further into the summer months the ramp becomes crowded, requiring an early arrival to find a parking spot.

Our last two points of interest are off Sandy Point. As you head down the channel you'll pass a series of green cans. Between the last can and the blinker off Sandy Point you'll see Ledwoods Island to the right. At that spot, just north of the river channel is a stretch of several submerged rocks. On a moving tide, the boils from water sweeping over the stones is easily spotted.

You'll also likely see a couple pot buoys. Position your boat to the side of the rocks, tossing plugs into them as the tide carries you along.

The dropoff around Sandy Point is our final destination. If you run in close to shore you'll notice how the sand drops away in some places like a cliff. When the tide sweeps around the edge, small bass to 30 pounders at times lie in wait. A plug or live bait worked here looks like the easy pickings it is. At various times during the season your plugs will be ambushed by small to medium blues as well as stripers. At other times nothing will await your efforts.

CHAPTER 5

Southwest Ledge — This Time Last Year

By this time last year most bluefishing reports were pointing to the end of the season. There were a few stragglers in the Sound; some still left at Cartwright and a few to the east of Block Island. Then a boat bound for bass at Block found Southwest Ledge to the southwest of Block Island's Southwest Point was full of choppers—big ones. Thanksgiving week brought tremendous catches to a handful of anglers who made the run out there.

The action had been on about a week when we got wind of it. Diamond jiggers were scoring on most days, while trollers were taking fish every tide. Some days, like November 20, the fish took the jigs on the drop, but wanted mostly trolled umbrellas on the flood. That day boats arriving in the morning trolled the high spots (marked on the charts) with rigs taking fish on the right passes. Get the rig down a shade too low and one or more of the hordes of dogfish in residence grabbed a tube or worse, became foul hooked. When the doggie came in tail first he'd wrap the rig in a horrible mess.

Boats squidding diamond and sand eel jigs off or on the high spots did very little that morning. Once in awhile, a jigging boat took a doggie, but nothing else. The fish were there; we'd mark them on the chart machine but diamond jigs didn't interest them.

What a difference an hour makes. The tide switched around to ebb and the jigs turned to pieces of candy. The fish hit them as they dropped down or grabbed them on the way back up. At times, every boat in the drift pattern was into fish. Some boats had four anglers apiece.

One addition providing more hookups was placing a surge tube on the rear of the jig. The flashing jig and spinning tube brought more strikes than just the plain jig. We had very good hit-to-hook-up ratio using 3/16" tubing instead of something thicker. The smaller tubing leaves more of the hook exposed thus you have a better chance of sticking a fish. Some surge tubes have very little hook protruding. These will cause you lost fish.

Another method of fishing the jig combines both trolling and jigging together. The idea is to put one wire rod out and troll normally. An angler on the other side can fish with a jig this way. Let the jig down but keep tension on the spool as the jig goes down. As soon as it hits, put the reel in gear. As you take slow turns, the jig will wobble slowly toward the surface. The forward motion of the boat causes this. This way you can pick blues laying at intermediate depths without varying the speed of the boat. The rig, on the other hand, is down at a pre-determined depth. The jig is working its way from the bottom on up. After the jig is halfway up, take the reel out of gear and let it go back down. Once it hits bottom, repeat the first procedure. Don't try this dropback variation when the boat turns. The jig on plain mono rod will tangle with the wire as it goes down.

If the fish show at SW Ledge again this year, be ready. The action was top shelf with plenty of elbow room. It was a far cry from the Race on sunny Sundays. Last year, the weather was superb. Put all three aspects together and it means keeping an eye on Southwest Ledge again this year.

Both trolling and jigging were working equally well.

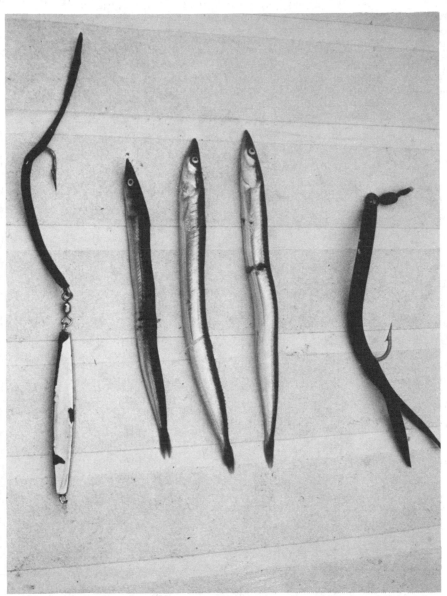

The hot lure that day and many since was a small diamond jig with a surge tube off the back.

John Baldino (on the right) is no stranger to big fish. A couple years ago he caught this 71 pound bass off Norwalk. While this bass was caught with bunker, John regularly fishes by trolling worms with his electric motor.

CHAPTER 6

Trolling Worms for Bass

John Baldino's name is not new to regular readers. Last year John came in first in our fishing contest with, among others, a 20 lb. bluefish and 71 lb. bass. At the time, the bass was one pound away from a world's record.

In 1981 John's name appeared under the Norwalk report section, particularly in July. During that month he and other regulars tallied some nice bass scores on bunker and trolled sandworms. I'd always wanted to do a story on worm trolling; seeing John's fish in the reports convinced me he was a good man to talk to.

John has lived in Norwalk all his life—fished there, too. He knows the chain of islands outside the harbor to be the right place on the right wind and tide. Knowing where is John's secret. We can, however, give you his methods. He fishes out of a well-worn 15' glass boat with 70 horse Evinrude. That gets him from harbor to island in about 15 minutes. The power for worm trolling comes from a portable electric trolling motor mounted on the stern. The motor is fed by a spare, deep cycle battery. Running at slow speeds, the battery will hold all night if necessary. After that it needs recharging.

His tackle for worms are spinning rods, about eight-footers, made up from Ugly Stik blanks. They have progressive tapers with sensitive tips, yet a lot of power in the butt section. Reels are Penn or Daiwa with 15 to 20 lb. test Maxima.

Whole, fresh sandworms are the bait. Most regulars buy worms by the flat for this type fishing. John keeps the leftovers in a porous laundry bag with drawstring top. He dumps both worms and seaweed in the bag after fishing, then lowers it over the side. When he goes again, he'll pick out the dead ones, then dump worms in a cardboard worm box (with fresh newspaper on the bottom). How long the worms live in the bag depends on the weather. The hotter, the less chance they have.

Hooks for worm trolling are #2 Eagle Claw bait holders. It's small, so small you have a tough time finding it when buried in the head of a sandworm. So does a bass. Yet the small hook will hold big fish. Above schoolie size, bass just suck the whole worm in. Schoolies might whack it a couple times, but most get the point. You want to run the hook about the length of the shank into the head of the worm. Leave the point exposed and the worm hanging straight down in a natural manner. Tie the mono right to the hook (no leader).

Baldino fishes a very tight drag. The island's shore lines are covered with boulders from boat to football size. Big fish all too often cut you off. Making them work for every bit of line they get somewhat reduces the chance of that happening. When it does you either go after them with the boat, or try again with a fresh rig. John recalled following numerous fish in the 30s this way and that, trying to unravel line from several different rocks. In the dark, this is easier said than done.

To present the worm, John lets out about 75' to 100' of line. He clicks on the trolling motor, then slowly creeps his way along the shore. The tighter in you are, the better you are. Keep in mind all his fishing is done in Long Island Sound. The islands are subject to wind and tide, but there's not much surf unless a stiff wind comes up.

Many times during the two nights we fished together, John's boat bumped into the numerous rocks. He once remarked if you are in more than fifteen feet of water, go to something besides worms. At one point, we hooked a fish just as the lower unit touched bottom in two feet of water. Big fish in season are in that close under cover of night. John's biggest so far this season, a fish in the low 40s, was taken in knee deep water.

John keeps the lower unit of his gas engine in the water to act as a rudder. By turning the motor this way or that he can maneuver the boat in or away from shore. If a breeze prevents him from making the slow headway he desires, he'll run upwind, then troll down with the electric. If wind that night blows parallel to the shore, use Mother Nature's propulsion. If the wind speed is somewhere between the two, use the electric motor in spurts. Remember, the worm only has a small hook in it. That's not much weight. Chances of it sinking to the bottom are greatly reduced.

When someone who has never trolled worms before goes with John, he has them fish the rod dead in the holder. Fish, even schoolies, the better part of the time, will hook themselves. Once the rod goes over, you have him. One charter boat captain who used to troll live bait did the same thing. A couple of John's partners keep the bail of the reel open. When a fish hits, they give it some line just as in drifting with a live eel. John fishes with open bail, but keeps his finger on the line. As soon as he feels the fish has the bait in his mouth, he sets up but does NOT give any slack. It's a method he's comfortable with. Why argue with success?

The first night we went out a storm blew us back in. Two weeks later, under a full moon, we got out again. The big fish, though, were gone for most; water temps were high. Schoolies were still in the neighborhood, but thank goodness, we weren't bothered by hordes of snapper blues. They sometimes raise havoc with worm trolling during a summer moon. We fished from 9 p.m. to 1 a.m., taking five small fish. All but one was let go. John uses a net to land the little guys so as not to harm them. His fishing club and a couple local tackle shop owners have been preaching release of the juveniles. It's the future of bass fishing.

Any time we run stories like this we get a couple letters saying so and so fished worms for 35 years, but not this way. That may be. It may also be both parties get their share. Lots of people disagree on rigging eels, yet a lot catch bass with their different techniques. It's often that way with other methods, like worm trolling.

CHAPTER 7

Flatfishing Around
The Mystic River

From a Boat

Some of our readers are now out surf fishing, but others are planning trips for flats. If you don't want to go all the way to Quincy, here's some suggestions for a location a lot closer to home. The Mystic River—and spots close by—has always been a productive area for flats. This fall is no exception.

First we'll take a look at places to fish from a boat and then a couple spots to stay along the shore. It would greatly help if you had the chart for Fisher's Island Sound by your chair or desk as you read the article. The chart will save you a lot of time looking for the spots once the weekend or day off rolls around.

Credit for most of the information in the story should go to Cliff at Shaffer's Boat Livery. Cliff has lived in this area all his life and knows the river very, very well. Now, let's get started. Run your finger all the way up the Mystic River to the very top of the chart. You should be able to make out the twin bridges of I-95 spanning the river. Off to the south, there's some dotted lines indicating the end of the deep water of the river channel. Right on the edge of the deep water is a good spot. This location is just off the Elm Grove Cemetery on the east bank. This spot is generally better later on in the fall and in the very early spring. As the water warms, the fish will move from the I-95 bridges down river of Murphy Point. Both these landmarks are designated as such on the chart. Between buoy 30 and the bridge, on the eastern edge of the channel, a lot of little flats are being caught as this is being written. This is a good spot to check after the fish start moving down river from up by the cemetery. To the north of the RR bridge, but on the western edge of the channel, is another spot worth a little time. Anchor up on the side, out of the way of all the boat traffic.

Due west of Murphy Point is a small unmarked cove with another RR bridge over it. The chart I have shows two feet of water there, but Cliff said it is deeper. On days with a strong northwest wind, people often anchor in close to the bridge. Not only do they get fish, but also get out of the cold wind. Bear in mind, anywhere along the channel can produce flats. The spots you are reading about seem to be better bets than just dunking a worm any ol' place.

Moving down river, we come to Sixpenny Island with buoy 19 at the tip closest to the channel. Here's a good spot on both tides, though Cliff said a lot of his customers like to fish here on the incoming. Further west of Sixpenny Island sits Beebe Cove. Water entering and exiting the cove on a moving tide does so underneath a RR bridge. Around the bridge is a deep cut that is sometimes full of flats. This is also a good spot for bass fishing. During May, some early fish over thirty pounds have been taken here at night with live buckies.

From Beebe Cove, we'll jump across to Mason's Island. On the southern tip of the Island, you'll see Mason Point and to the east of that, Baker Island. In between Baker Island and Cormorant Reef (to the east) you'll see buoy 6. To the south of that buoy, in ten to fifteen feet of water, is a spot to hit in the

One popular spot for shorefishing for flounders is under the I-95 bridge over the Mystic River. All fishing is done on the west bank as the east side is private property.

late spring or early fall. Any moving tide will produce fish if they're in residence.

Now we have to jump across the Sound to Fisher's Island. If you want to stop along the way and try for blacks, there's good numbers at buoy 19 at a reef called Middle Clump. Try around fifteen feet of water on the incoming tide. If you don't want to stop, then any of the coves on the north side of Fisher's Island have flats in them.

From Shore

There are many places to fish from shore along the river, but a lot of them we can't advertise. We can say if you don't make a mess, you can probably fish off a lot of the boat docks without too many hassles. The following are the better known spots reachable without any fuss.

One popular spot is the Mason's Island bridge. To get here, continue on Greenmanville Avenue (Route 27). Follow this through to Route #1. Take a left and stay on Route #1 until the first traffic light. Make a right here onto Masons Island Road. Follow it about a mile-and-a-half to the bridge. Any moving tide is good.

One last place to try is under the I-95 bridge over the Mystic River on the west bank. The east bank is private property. This is a very popular spot, and you can park next to where you are fishing. To reach here, get off I-95 at Exit 89. Coming from the east, take a right at the top of the ramp. Take a left coming from the west. Take a right to Cow Hill Road and follow this to Bindloss Road. Take a left there to River Road, then take a right. The fishing area is in around the supports to the bridge. You can pull off on the shoulder, get out and start fishing. Later on in the fall and early spring are your best times here.

The Mason's Island bridge is another popular spot. It's accessible through the Town of Mystic via Mason's Island Road.

CHAPTER 8

Plugging Bass off Milford

A carpenter works with wood, a plumber with pipe, a mason with stone and Bob Mahoney with an Atom Junior or a rigged eel. Unlike the first three, Bob doesn't make his living with those "tools" but he puts in enough hours chasing bass that you might think he was earning his keep. You the reader or me the writer would certainly smile generously if somebody gave either of us one dollar for every hour Bob's spent bobbing around in the Sound between the mouth of the Housatonic and Anchor Beach.

I met Bob at a recent meeting of the Milford Striped Bass Club. A couple times during the meeting somebody spoke of noteworthy bass. The name Mahoney usually followed the poundage. This happened enough times so I was more than happy to accept an invitation to fish with Bob after we struck up a conversation at the meeting.

Bob and his family live in Milford. Bob's job with the phone company is in the area and so are his bass. From the beginning of June through October Bob spends as much time on or near the water as he can. Bob's method of fishing is casting rigged eels or plugs from his anchored or drifting 19' MFG with a 60 horse Chrysler.

The night I fished with him we had dinner at the Mayflower Diner off Exit 40 then were off to the Milford Town ramp. By 9:30 p.m. we were on our way down the harbor.

After 15 puffs of Bob's cigar from the launching ramp the river widened just south of the first cluster of sailboats. Just below this pool the river swings to the south. When the bunkers are thick in the river Bob has seen some very hefty bass chasing bunkers in the still of the night right in this area.

Next spot Bob pointed out was the entrance of Gulf Pond into Milford Harbor. On the dropping tide a rip forms at the intersection of the two bodies of water. The water from Gulf Pond flows under a bridge before it enters the harbor. On the northeast corner of the bridge is a sandbar. At low water the bar is exposed. You can wade this bar on a dropping tide to catch school bass feeding in the rip. Rebel plugs work nicely.

The night before we fished it blew 25 mph from the southeast. It was too rough to go outside so Bob caught a decent mess of school fish by the bridge.

After we cleared the number four can outside the harbor entrance we swung to the southwest toward Welches Point. Welches is one of Bob's favorite spots. In years past it's produced on both tides.

We anchored about 75 feet south of the apex of the point just as the tide started ebbing. Bass favor the pocket formed by the breakwater jutting out to the southeast and the point itself. We flipped plugs in all directions from the boat but only had hits casting toward the breakwater in an east/northeast direction from the boat.

I used an amber Atom 40; Bob had on his favorite: a white Atom Junior. Give Mr. Mahoney only one lure to use the rest of his life and he said he'd choose the Atom Junior. That's quite a compliment for a plug.

By the time Bob caught and released his second bass I switched to a Junior. We cast for another two hours. Bob had another fish smack the plug twice on consecutive casts but missed him both times. My partner for the night said he only fishes after dark because of the elbow room. That night we fished six of Bob's pet spots without seeing another fisherman. Most of Bob's fishing is done Monday through Thursday. At say 3 a.m. on Wednesday only a few sharpshooter-type fishermen are out.

The moon stage doesn't interest Bob that much with the exception of the full moon. He's never done much under the bright moon unless it was rough.

Best wind is one that puts a 6 to 10 inch chop on the Sound. "That ol' Atom really shines" under those conditions said Bob. When it's flat Bob bends the front eye of the Junior way down so it creates a V wake as it rides along the surface.

If one were to plug along the Milford shoreline with Rebels, bass will oblige on most nights. Speaking of Rebels, Bob and a friend named John each caught a bass in the thirties at Welches while casting from the shore on either side of a fellow using a Rebel. Bob and John used rigged eels. The fellow with the Rebel had been fishing the spot before the pair arrived but didn't have a fish to his name. Bob and John stepped in and both had their bass on the beach in short order.

We took a break casting so Bob showed me a Junior literally broken from the thrashing of a bass hooked right in the spot we were in. The styrofoam had cracked right through to the wire between the second and last set of trebles. The trebles themselves were bent out of shape.

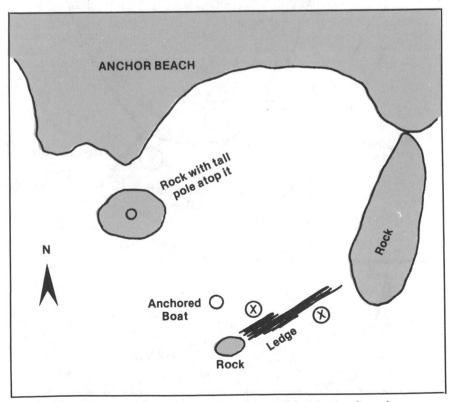

The Xs with circles around them mark the locations where bass were hooked.

Biggest bass Bob has taken in this area was 59 pounds. He has several other fifties to his credit—all from the same general area. The 59 pounder hit at Anchor Beach which is where we headed after the tide got halfway down.

If you look on chart 218 you will see Anchor Beach is labeled Merwin Point. From Merwin Beach to Merwin Point there are four points of land jutting out. Between the third point (going west to east) and the first rock to the south of it was where we anchored. We put the boat in about 100 feet to the northwest of that southern rock.

We cast between the rock and the shore; no hits that night but Bob has done well here. Come to think of it, Bob has done well in most spots he fishes at one time or another.

To get to the next stop we ran between the southern rock and the shore. We anchored up about 200 feet to the southwest of a big rock with a tall pole atop it. To the southeast of our boat was another smaller rock sticking above water. Between that rock and the shore is a ledge that runs southwest to northeast. Our Atom Juniors were cast back toward the ledge.

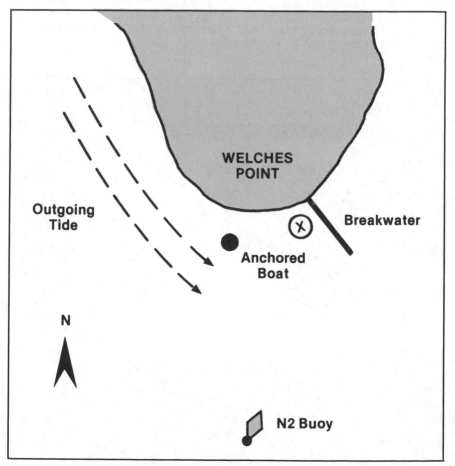

X with a circle around it marks the approximate location of feeding bass. That could obviously change from day to day.

The two bass we caught hit as the plugs were about to go over or away from the ledge. Bob's fish was a rat that thrashed so much on the surface it tired itself out then and there. My bass went 12-14 pounds. It grabbed the plug ever so lightly then dove, pulling the line over a rock. My line was at a 90 degree angle to the fish when he came out of the water. He swam by three more rocks before we returned plug and fish to the boat. Thanks to 30 pound mono on conventional gear we got the fish. I doubt if such would have happened with 15 pound line on a spin outfit.

It looked like we'd interested the only eaters in the area so we went to Point Beach. Off Point Beach there's a rock sticking out of the water at half tide. We scooted between the rock and the shore to cast plugs as the boat drifted west to east. Nobody got any hits.

Next stop was Charles Island. Bob went in about 300 feet from the southernmost tip of the island. Again, we cut the motor then cast the Juniors. Lockjaw in this spot too; last stop was the mouth of the Housatonic.

The end of the outgoing tide at the mouth of the river was what Bob wanted. He said bass that moved up into the river to feed on the flood would be dropping out on the last part of the ebb. We pulled up to about 500 feet off Stratford Point. The boat had 3-4 feet of water under it. Bass often come up on this flat to feed but not that night. We had all the fish we were going to get.

Back at the diner that coffee tasted g-o-o-d. We were both tired from six hours of fishing. Four fish to 12-14 pounds will never make the record books but that's the way bass fishing is. Some nights you can't even scrounge up 25 percent of that total, but you're right back after them the next night.

For me, the next night meant typing this story. I don't know for certain but I'm willing to bet if you were off Welches Point just after the tide started ebbing you'd hear the splat of an Atom Junior or rigged eel hitting the surface. More than likely Bob Mahoney was hard at work once again.

With two rods you can present two baits, giving you a chance to find out what's producing best on a given day. In addition, you might fish a bucktail with one rod and bait rig on the other.

CHAPTER 9

Two Rods for Fluke

Editor's Note: Last week we ran an article about fluke fishing outside the Mystic River. Well, it seems a lot of people were interested enough to get in touch about more info. What they primarily wanted was some more how-to, since most of the article dealt with where-to.

It is impossible to put all the necessary how-to into one, or even two stories. One suggestion I can make toward covering most possible topics is buying the Fluke book written by Don Kamienski. It's available from The Fisherman Library, 1622 Beaver Dam Road, Point Pleasant, N.J. 08742. Cost is $7.95.

Beyond the info in the book, I would add your fishing will be more productive if you use two rods. The reasons for this are many and varied depending on who you talk to. With two rods you present more than one bait to the fish. This gives you a chance to find out what's producing the best on any given day. After you've found the best item, put both rods to work with the top bait.

In addition to bait, you might want to try a lure on the second rod. A white bucktail sweetened with a strip of squid—at times—works better than anything you can put in the water. The dancing jig with the smell of squid draws a fluke's attention—again, at certain times—better than the bait drifting along the soft bottom.

The idea is to cut a strip of squid about four inches long. It should be tapered from top to bottom, from about a quarter inch down, to a fine pointed end. Hook the squid once through the middle of its widest part. Then lower the jig to the bottom and raise it slowly up and down. You want the lure to be down on the bottom each time it drops.

Fluke will hit the bucktail at times with authority. Just lift the rod to set the hook when this happens. At other times, they'll just hold onto the end of the squid. This will feel like you've picked up some extra weeds. You have to get into the habit of not being too quick. When you go to lift the bucktail—and feel weight—give a couple seconds pause before raising the lure. A fluke just might be on the other end, eating his way to the hook.

In a running tide, with a stiff breeze, you might have to go to three ounce bucktails to stay down. Fishing out in the deeper confines of the Sound or in open ocean, you might have to go as high as an eight ounce bucktail. The eight ouncer with a strip of squid is a heap of a thing to put in the water. However, it has the proven record of taking doormats in the ten to fourteen pound class out of deep water.

In sheltered bays, the bucktail combo often produces a passel of smaller fluke, while the bigger fish go for the bigger bait drifted along on the second rod. The point is you can increase your catch noticeably by catching smaller fish with the bucktail while "waiting" for bigger stuff.

Another reason for two rods is you can vary the type of tackle whenever possible. While drifting off Mason's Island on days with a moderate breeze, I found these conditions let me use light plug casting tackle for fluke. See the article "A Small Stick" in the 2/22/79 issue for specs. A four pound fish on this tackle is much more fun than standard bottom gear reserved for such fishing as Block Island cod. Under normal conditions with seventeen or twenty pound test line, I can usually get by with a half to an ounce-and-a-half bucktail or two ounce sinker if bait fishing with the light tackle.

When I use bait with the little rod, it is usually smaller bait. For instance, it might be a couple small herring on the little stick and a small, whole squid or smelt on the heavier tackle. The smaller baits bring more fish, but of a smaller size. It is the same story as the bucktail fishing. You "pass the time," hopefully catching a couple small fish while waiting for a bigger one to eat the bigger bait.

Unless you are like my friend Patrick who fishes two rods at once (one in each hand), you will likely hold one rod and lay the other down against the gunwale. As you drift along, notice how the dead rod's tip moves as the sinker works along the bottom. This might take a few moments of study. After you've determined what is the "standard" rod tip action, pay close attention to any deviation from the "norm."

A slight extra dip might be a piece of grass or it just might be an eight pounder. When you pick up the dead rod and feel extra weight on the other end, pay out a couple feet of line. What you are doing is giving the fluke time to get the bait in his mouth. Next time you lift the rod, be on the lookout for a wiggle or other signs of life. If there isn't any, it probably means you've just given a ball of weeds time to "eat" your bait. If there is some action, set the hook with a slow upward sweep of the rod.

The habit of fluke to slowly take a bait is a good reason to put a bigger bait on the second rod laying dead on the gunwale. The dormant stick reduces the chance of an over-eager angler pulling the bait away from a nice fish. This means even a bigger fluke has a chance to get the bigger bait to a point where the hook does some good.

With the two rod setup, be prepared for the unexpected. With two baits drifting along side-by-side it is not uncommon for one fluke to grab both of them. If you use a bucktail on the second rod, a weakfish might end up in the fish box. If you drift from sand bottom to the edge of some rocks, a sea bass or two might eat your offering. Like I said before, the two rods will put more fish in the boat at the end of the day.

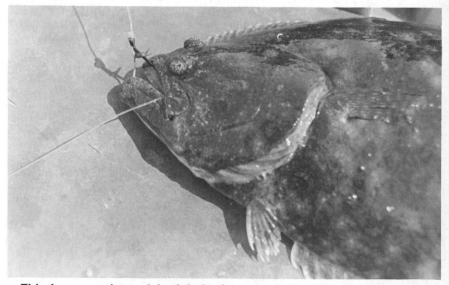

This four pounder took both baits from two different rods. It was caught off the tip of Mason's Point.

CHAPTER 10

Build a Bluefish Rod

Normally we run rod building articles during the winter layover. But, never an organization that puts much to do on tradition (just ask someone who works in our office), we thought you might like to get a rod ready for the fall, which, by the way, is fast approaching.

The specs on the opposite page are mainly for light tackle people. It's a seven footer that will take quite awhile with a 15 pounder. If you want quantity, just skip over this story. This bluefish rod will not be everybody's bluefish rod.

It is best suited to fishing single hook diamond jigs with a speedy retrieve, a method commonly referred to as speed squidding. We've run many articles in the past dealing with the how-to of it all. Basically, you drop a jig anywhere from 2 to 8 oz. to bottom, then crank like hell. If there are no hits, drop the jig back down, and repeat the procedure. Speed squidding is not the best way to locate fish; that's better left to trolling. Once you find them stacked up some place, put the jigs to work. Catching big blues with this tackle is a lot more fun than something with capable of besting a 400 lb. mako.

All the specs are laid out in bold, clear type. The blanks don't have to be cut, and they are ones readily available to anyone close to a good source of rod materials. It's not something exotic only one company in the country carries.

Reels to go along with this rod would be Shimano, Garcia 6500, Penn 940, Newell 200, etc. Lines would normally be anywhere from 12 to 20 lbs. If you are new to any light tackle fishing, I'd recommend the 20 pound line.

Editor's Note: All rod specs courtesy of J&B Tackle Company.

—BLANKS—

Use a Lamiglas MB841E or WB841E, or a Fenwick SP846. All three blanks are seven foot long. Do not cut; use as is. The Fenwick is a bit lighter. The Lamiglas MB blank is yellow while the WB is white.

—REEL SEATS & GRIPS—

Use a Fuji FPS #20 or 7/8" chrome on brass. The latter reel seat is less expensive. Most builders today use hypalon grips. This rod takes an eight inch butt grip and five inch for grip plus a one inch butt cap.

—GUIDE SPACING—

Use seven Fuji BNHG guides and a #7 Fuji BPHT top.

From tip to 1st guide — 3½"	From 5th to 6th guide — 9½"
From 1st to 2nd guide — 4½"	From 6th to 7th guide — 10"
From 2nd to 3rd guide — 6"	From 7th guide to
From 3rd to 4th guide — 7½"	center of reel seat — 21½"
From 4th to 5th guide — 9¼"	

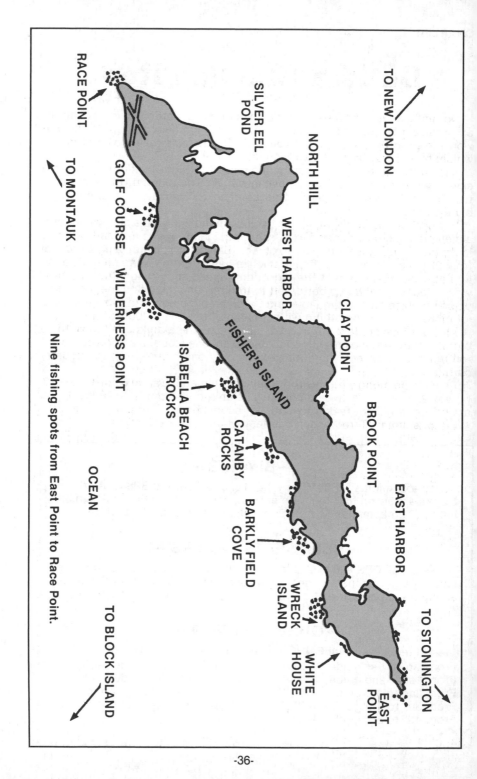

TO NEW LONDON

RACE POINT

SILVER EEL POND

NORTH HILL

TO MONTAUK

GOLF COURSE

WEST HARBOR

CLAY POINT

WILDERNESS POINT

FISHER'S ISLAND

BROOK POINT

EAST HARBOR

ISABELLA BEACH ROCKS

CATANBY ROCKS

OCEAN

BARKLY FIELD COVE

WRECK ISLAND

WHITE HOUSE

TO STONINGTON

EAST POINT

TO BLOCK ISLAND

Nine fishing spots from East Point to Race Point.

-36-

CHAPTER 11

The Oceanside of Fisher's Island

Fourteen years ago it was time to realize a boyhood ambition to live and work near some of the better bass holes on the New England Coast. After leaving the University of Rhode Island with a journalism degree, *The Fisherman* magazine and I found ourselves working in Mystic, Ct., while I found a house in Westerly, R.I. Among the many places to explore were the Watch Hill Reefs, the famous rips of the Race and the oceanside of Fisher's Island, some of the best casting water you'll find.

Over the years much was written about the famous bass islands like Cuttyhunk and the Vineyard while Fisher's has been relegated to somewhat lesser status. But, if you talk to the steadies you'll find Fisher's Island was the scene of some extremely good fishing during the most recent heyday of the striped bass, the early to mid 70s. Besides the quantity of fish, some of the stripers hit the 55 to 65 plus range; some of the fish were likely world record opportunities. As with other famous bass hideouts from Wicopesset Island to Old Silas Rock in the Sluiceway, I suspect some of the Fisher's Island regulars fought and lost battles with fish in excess of 70 pounds.

Today, however, most of the live bait fleet of the 70s is gone, having taken up other pursuits since the moratoriums and no sale laws went into effect. Fisher's Island isn't gone; it's still there offering angling opportunities for those willing to take a boat out along its south or oceanside looking to catch a bass or bluefish.

Fisher's Island lies off the eastern end of Connecticut between Stonington and New London separated from the mainland by Fisher's Island Sound. By some twist in history the island belongs to New York State so it's possible, since New York recently went to one fish over 33 inches per day, for an angler or his son or daughter to keep a trophy bass should they be fortunate to catch one. There's also an ever-increasing amount of school bass, perfect for light tackle fishing and a summer population of various size blues that come and go with bait movements. If you put all three together with an angler willing to put in his time, you have the formula for some enjoyable time afloat.

Without a doubt the best way to fish the island is with some type of live bait. If that interests you, look into the many articles we've run over the years on this subject. If you're the type willing to cast lures (an honorable pastime, though no competition for a wiggling pogy), then read on. All locations listed will produce at one time or another for both bait or artificials.

My two loves for fishing the island are an ultralight spinning rod with 4 pound line and three inch Rapalas or heavy duty spinning or conventional suited to toss the largest size Danny surface swimmers. These big lures are 8 inches long and waddle along the top with a V wake. Jumbo blues will try to bite them in half as will a respectable number of 20 to 35 lb. stripers. I've never landed a truly monster fish on the plugs from Fisher's Island, but have seen some Toyota sized swirls from a couple areas. One evening a friend of mine had a nice fish at Wreck Island knock the plug completely out of the water.

A usual evening behind the island might start off with the small spinner trying for schoolies. Last season we landed them up to 11 lbs. and will keep looking for that 20 pounder on four. However, once the sun dips behind the rim of the land, it's time to bring out the heavy stuff in hopes Mama is home. The big lures are particularly effective on days of calm to moderate surf. If the weather is up and pounding, don't look for me or my little boat back there. Keep the retrieve of the plug steady for the most, but once during each retrieve come back hard on the rod to make the lure splash water. Sometimes, when a finicky fish has swirled once but will not come back, this maneuver makes up her mind.

If you have some time on your hands that night you just might bring along a bucket of live eels. If you've marked a spot with big fish at sunset, go back in there after dark with the live bait. You'll probably have to work your way through the blues as they whack the eels into cigar butts, but the fisherman who persists will catch some large blues and a yearly score of larger bass.

You can fish behind the island from the end of May right through sometime in November and reasonably expect a chance at a good fish. My own timetable calls for fishing the island about mid to end of June through the end of September. Before and after that is time for bass in other areas. People lucky enough to live on the island start catching schoolies sometime between the beginning of May and the full moon. Some are still going towards the moon in November.

As one looks over the chart of the oceanside of Fisher's you'll see any number of shoreline nooks and crannies that might hold fish. To help out people who want to fish in the 1980s when one fish per trip is the rule, the following is a rundown of some of the better holes on the island's south shore.

Number One: East Point. Down on the eastern tip you'll see a real live castle that used to belong to the family who owned Simmons Mattresses. As you approach the castle from the east, take a moment to see a couple large boulders awash. On the last hour or so of the incoming tide and sometimes into slack water we've had fish here. One night I flipped a swimmer in there to have a true jumbo get off after wrenching hooks I felt were impregnable. One note of caution: on the strength of the incoming, the tide screams through here so until you get the lay of the land, the slower tides are easier to fish and much safer.

Number Two: White House. As you motor to the west along the first third of the shore you'll notice a white house on a bluff just to the east of Wreck Island. Here's another place we've had action while casting; this includes some teen sized blues on quiet nights. Make sure you pitch the lures right up into the stones.

Number Three: Wreck Island. Off the west of the island is a finger of sunken rocks that juts out in roughly a north to south line. On the seaward edge of the rocks is a large sunken boulder that breaks in all but the calmest weather. We call your attention to the seaward edge of the rock as some nice fish have come out of that locale. If you find yourself in this section as the sun drops behind the land it might be wise to anchor up a bit up-tide and offshore to toss swimmers into the swirls made by waves breaking over the boulder. Sometimes the fish will not show until last light or thereafter. If sunset is at 8PM, the next hour to hour and a half is prime time.

Number Four: Barley Field Cove. Boat fishermen might do well to concentrate on the apex of the rocks that form a rough semi-circle around the cove. Right off the point of the rocks is one place I've seen some large fish come up for a look at the Big Danny. Larger blues sometimes prowl here and will gladly eat the small Rapala that is thrown their way. If you find bait concentrated here but don't do anything that evening, try coming back at daybreak for a possible pleasant surprise.

Number Five: Catanby Rocks. The water here is as fishy as one could want, even on some days when you hit slack water on the month's slower tides. Try casting either size lure into the front of the rocks jutting out or into the formations that dot the shoreline just to the west. People with chart machines will find a nice hump off those shoreline rocks.

Number Six: Isabella Beach Rocks. On the shoreline of sandy Isabella Beach you can look to the east until you run into a rocky area with small stream entering the ocean along the western edge of the rocks. Readers who fish in this primo spot can cast to the rocks just around the stream entrance or work the surf just to the east. As you drift along the shore look off to the southwest and you'll note a moving tide swirling about a reef just offshore. The inside section of the reef is castable water too. If you or I had $100 for every jumbo fish landed from Isabella Beach, we'd be reading and writing about wahoo fishing from our condos in the Bahamas.

Number Seven: Wilderness Point. The rocks just below the point are choice holding areas as is the corner where the shoreline bends back in toward the island. If you've got a southwest breeze with incoming tide I'd very much recommend you make more than one toss with the big swimmer right at the corner. The area off Wilderness, in the better days of bass fishing, was frequented by one of the finest anglers I ever had the pleasure to speak with. He lived in Narragansett and fished the waters from Cuttyhunk to the Sluiceway in a 16', red Starcraft. People who've fished awhile know who I mean.

Number Eight: Golf Course Rocks. Not as productive as some other areas but they hold fish from time to time. If you're faced with calm water some evening with an incoming tide you might lay off and cast in here. This is a shallower spot compared with other rock piles, but the sand eels do gather.

Number Nine: Race Point Rocks. On the outgoing tide, waters from Long Island Sound swirl between here and Race Point Light. Casters can motor up to the rocks from the south, being watchful of boulders awash, then flip a plug into the current coming across the shallower sections of the point. Blues with some bass lay in wait to catch the bait. Sometimes you'll see charter boats trolling short wires just outside the rocks in the 15 to 18 foot depths just off the stones. This same range was also good at times for small boat fishing the tube and worm combo. People leery of their outdrives should investigate at low water some calm day, then try the last couple hours of the outgoing. At times the bluefish casting here can be quite good with various size fish at different times of the year. When this area is crashing, it's no place for someone just getting started.

Fisher's Island isn't a location where a 50 lb. bass lurks behind each boulder. It's like any other rocky stopover where bass and blues move about in search of a summer meal. If you give it more than a passing glance, you'll be in a position to enjoy the fruits of your labors. The fish are there waiting for you to come find them.

The late Danny Pichney (on the right), maker of the Danny plug, and Captain Don Lynch with a school fish plugged off Cuttyhunk.

CHAPTER 12

To Cast for Bass

Editor's Note: This week we bring you some locations to consider if you like to cast for bass and blues. Please be cautioned all these spots have broken bottom. Rocks are awash or, in some cases, just below the surface. One should not go charging in until you know the lay of the land. A couple trips in daylight on a calm day before attempting fishing at night seems prudent. Outdrives and lower units are not getting any cheaper. On all the diagrams the circles with Xs inside them are choice areas. It should also be noted the circled locales are not the only places in that area where fish lay or move in to feed.

Diagram #1: Cuttyhunk has "almost" more plugging spots than our budget has red ink. Two of the many places are in Canapitsit Channel and near the beached barges; both of these are on the eastern tip of the island. The rocks near the nun buoy are effectively fished only during slack water. Once the tide gets rolling, try some place else. The other area is to the southeast of the barge. Rocks awash bend in toward the shore, forming a pocket. Fish the outside edge of the pocket.

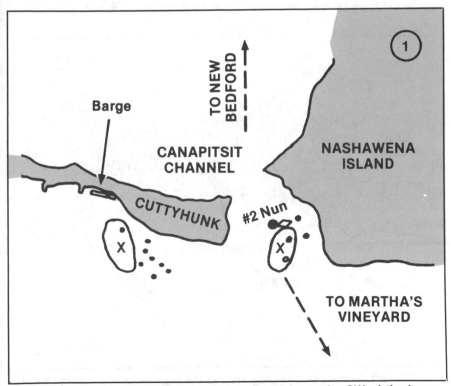

Two good locations at Cuttyhunk are the rocks to the SW of the barge and near the #2 nun in Canapitsit Channel.

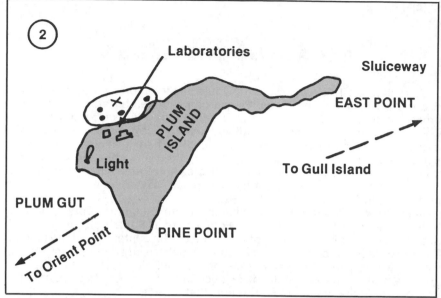

During slack water or slower tides you can plug in and around the sunken boulders off the laboratories on the north side of Plum Island.

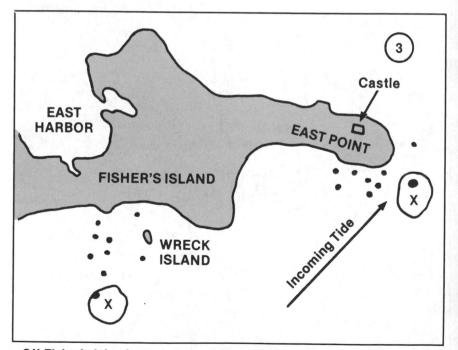

Off Fisher's Island you can plug around the big rock awash off to the SE of East Point. The last hour of the incoming tide is best here. There's another big rock awash to the SW of Wreck Island which can also be productive.

Diagram #2: Some night or at daybreak, if the tide is slack, you might try plugging the north side of Plum Island around the laboratories. Please be extra careful in here as there are numerous rocks awash just waiting to fight with your boat. On calm nights some people spend slack tide here casting eels. Others troll the deeper water outside the rocks and on some tides have done very well. Be cautious.

Diagram #3: There's a lot of little nooks and crannies on the ocean side of Fisher's Island that hold bass. These two are but a drop in the bucket. Just outside the eastern point of the island is a large rock off to the southeast. This rock sits out by itself. On the end of the incoming tide or during slack water is a good time to fish here. Wreck Island is another decent spot. The rock just under the surface (circled) off to the southwest of the island usually has a bass around it, if the fish are around.

Diagram #4: Menunketesuck Island lies off the Town of Westbrook near the mouth of the Menunketesuck River. It's a thin, scraggy-looking piece of real estate running north to south. Best fishing is on the southern tip of the island on an outgoing tide. There you will find three breaks in the rocks. Through each of these breaks goes the tide, creating small rips on the eastern side. Those rips are prime spots as is the large pointed rock which is the last rock sticking clear of the water as one moves to the south away from the island.

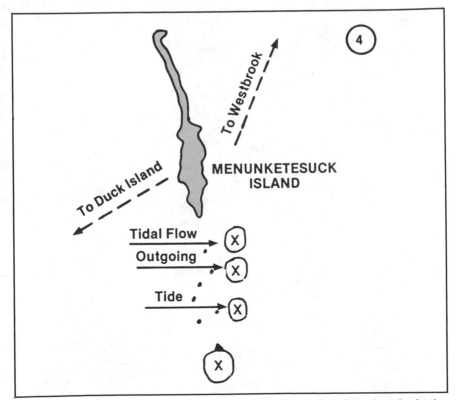

On the south end of Menunketesuck Island you'll find three breaks in the reef. On an outgoing tide, each one of those breaks (on the down-tide side) may hold fish at different stages of the tide.

Where's the best possible blackfish spot in Connecticut waters? Serious consideration would have to be given to Southwest Reef off Westbrook as the top contender.

CHAPTER 13

Is Southwest the Best?

One of the last games in town for the small boat fisherman in Long Island Sound is blackfishing. Here and there, from Greenwich all the way up to Stonington, guys will be out as LATE as weather permits, seeking a mess of tautog.

Where's the best possible spot in the whole State of Connecticut? By no means have I fished all the areas. However, based on the info gotten in six years of dealing with most of the tackle stores, I'd say Southwest Reef (both inner and outer) off Duck Island near the Town of Westbrook, would have to get serious consideration as the top blackfish producer anywhere in Connecticut waters.

There just doesn't seem to be any end to the tautog on both these reefs. For instance, Phil "VFW" Wetmore and myself had 563 pounds one tide in October. A week later, we had 263 pounds and two days after that, ol' VFW had slightly over 300 pounds all by his lonesome. In-between trips, plenty of other boats did well, too. Jim at the Outdoorsman in Clinton could give you plenty of names of people doing well there. John Racci and partners usually took between 200 and 300 pounds each trip out. Bear in mind this is only the tip of the iceberg. Think about all the fish no one ever hears about!

I and O (inner and outer SW reefs) are located to the southwest of the #6 buoy to the south of Duck Island. Inner is about one-and-a-quarter nautical miles out. Inner is easy to spot. It is marked on the charts and is usually dotted with lobster pots plus being marked by a fairly well-defined rip, especially when the wind is against the tide. Outer is not marked on a chart. It is the piece of forty foot water to the south of inner. Look for the numbers 43 to 46 on a chart. That's the top part of the reef.

Both green and hermit crabs will take fish here. Try a two-hook rig: if you miss the first hit, you have another bait right in place to maybe stick him the second time around.

A lot of blackfishermen have certain set times they prefer to fish. A majority seem to favor the slower tides at beginning and end of slack water. The day we took the 263 pounds, we had poor fishing on the end of the incoming and slack water. We were on the outer reef. A couple of the blackfish pros that hang around Christy's Restaurant, however, did well on the slack, only they fished inner. We got most of our fish as the outgoing tide picked up strength. On that moon-tide day, though, we had to go to heavy weights; then heavy weights with wire line to stay down. The tide ran so hard, twenty ounces of lead would NOT hold bottom before the first hour of the tide had passed. We went to thirty-two ounces on mono and held up until the second hour. Dacron line was **no** good at all because of the drag. As long as we could hold the crabs down stationary on the bottom, fish hit in a steady stream. About two-and-a-half hours into the fast tide, we switched to forty ounces and continued to take fish. Another boat a short ways away wasn't doing nearly as well. I suspect his bait was moving too much in the swift flow. At the top of the tide, even forty ounces wasn't enough. We broke out a wire line outfit, tied a four foot mono leader to the end of the wire, tied a bait rig to the leader and dropped it over with forty ounces. The current hummed past the wire, but the rig stayed in place. We continued to catch fish, thanks to the wire.

It is possible to catch fish at all stages of the tide out on those reefs. On some days, though, you have to go to extremes to stay on the bottom. Incidentally, two weeks after the tautog wire line episode, I talked with a commercial rod and reeler fishing out of Nauset Inlet. He was using sixty pound wire and twenty-seven ounce jigs to stay near the bottom in 130' of water while codfishing. He tried seventy-seven ounces of weight to stay down with mono. It didn't work. The tide lifted the 4.6 pounds of weight away from the strike zone. After switching to the wire, he fished productively. The total for two men for two days was 700-plus pounds the first trip, and a little shy of 1,000 the second day out.

The season is fast coming to a close for a lot of our readers. If you want one more shot with your own boat, there's Southwest Reef off Westbrook. "Toetogs" there are plentiful and stubborn when it comes to getting them up off the bottom. About the only thing more stubborn to move than a big blackfish is my friend, Phil, from his cold beer on a hot day while he's politickin' from a stool at the VFW Post.

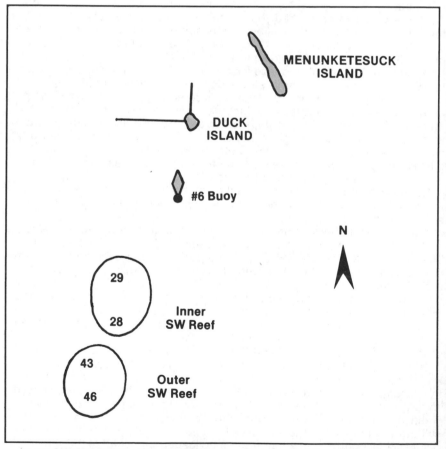

Inner SW Reef is in about 30 feet of water about 1¼ miles SW of the #6 buoy off Duck Island. The outer part of the reef is 45 to 50 foot deep and roughly 1¼ to 2 miles south of the buoy.

CHAPTER 14

Mini Umbrella Rig

A pain in the gluteus maximus is the way some fishermen look on the umbrella rig, especially the bigger varieties. Six arm rigs with as many as thirteen hooks, covering a diameter as much as twenty-eight inches are awkward to fish with—not to mention storing on a small boat. Because of those facts, some anglers refuse to use the rigs in spite of their proven potential.

Fishing tackle manufacturers are always bringing out new products based on the needs of the fishing public. For the last couple seasons, there has been a much smaller, compact umbrella rig on the market. This mini rig does catch fish and it's a breeze to store and fish with compared to the bulkier models.

The Fisherman first reported the trend to smaller rigs in an article in our 8/18/77 issue. That story was prompted by the success of a new breed of rig being used off Point Judith Lighthouse to take school bass feeding on a large school of sand eels. Fishermen like Captain Fred Gallagher and very good fishermen from the Cape took fish everyday on the small umbrellas. The rigs had arms measuring six inches from the centerpiece to the outside of tip of the arm. The diameter of this rig was twelve to thirteen inches, much smaller than the standard sizes previously mentioned.

Those smaller rigs were used in conjunction with 3/16" black latex tubing instead of the standard 7/16". The smaller diameter tubing seems to work well with the smaller rigs. We'll get into the rigging of the tubes in just a sec or so. First the rig itself.

After seeing that smaller umbrella in action, I started checking tackle stores to find out what I'd been missing. A search up into the Massachusetts area revealed several stores carrying the items. In a couple places, they had even smaller rigs than the ones Freddy and his partner used. Those mini rigs were the ones I got interested in.

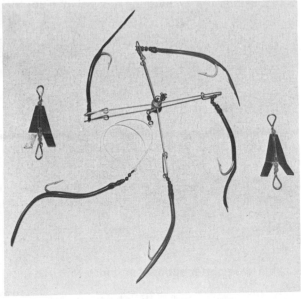

Mini umbrella rig measures only six inches from the centerweight to outside tip of each arm. Some people find this much easier to fish than bulkier standard size rigs.

The mini rig is manufactured by Zing Products, P.O. Box 1407, Fall River, Mass. 02722. The arms measure three-and-a-half inches from the center-piece to tip, giving a diameter of seven inches. The arms are made of spring steel so they will withstand the pressure of double-bubble blues or bass. Besides holding up to the strains of hard fishing the rigs store easily thanks to their reduced size.

Four rigs with four tubes on the end of each arm and a trailer tube with leader going down the center can be stored in a plastic container measuring 7½" long, 5¼" wide and 3" high. The container was purchased in a supermarket where it was intended to be sold for storing foodstuffs in a refrigerator. Imagine having four umbrella rigs ready to use in a container the size of a shoebox. Such a container can be slipped under the console of a fishing boat without any storage problem whatsoever.

Now let's talk about setting the rig up. Because of the vast schools of sand eels around, I firmly believe that 3/16" tubing is the way to go. Lay a seven inch strip of this tubing next to a sand eel; that match-up in length and width will be almost identical. Pieces of tubing seven inches long will match up to the average size sand eels found on the inshore waters. Color is up to the individual angler. As a general note, black, white or green have been productive in the past.

Next, cut about a three inch section off one end of the tube by slicing the tubing at a 45° angle. You want the sliced end to taper to a fairly fine point. After cutting you should be able to see a tube cut down the middle from a point three inches from one end. That thin, wispy piece of tubing is impor-tant for reasons we'll get to shortly.

The cut piece of tubing can be slid up a 7/0 surge tube hook. These are sold in many, many tackle shops along the coast. If you have trouble sliding the tube up the hook, dip the tubing in some type of dishwashing liquid first. The liquid will act as a lubricator.

Once you get the tubing up near the shank of the hook—stop. Now you want to get a short piece of eighty pound bead chain. Insert one eye of the bead chain in the eye of the hook, then close the eye of the hook with a pair of pliers. Now slide the tubing up over the eye and the first ball or so of the

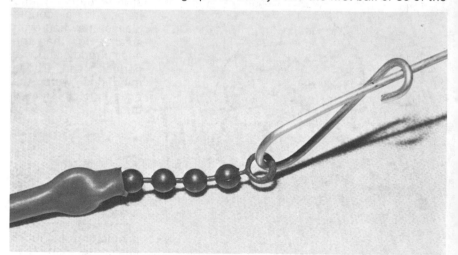

Tubes rigged with bead chain have better action than those with just two-way swivels.

links of bead chain.

Some anglers rig their tubes with barrel swivels, but bead chain with its free swiveling action enables the tubes to spin much easier. The easier spinning produces more action and fish. In addition, please remember the thin tail of tubing we just talked about. That will have plenty of action in the water as the tube moves freely on the bead chain.

At this point some anglers put spinners between the tubes and the arms of the rig. This choice is up to you. One thing to bear in mind: as you add the spinners, you increase the cost of the rig. Spinners catch the eye of the fish, but you have to pay for the added attractions. The mini rig takes four tubes—one for each of its arms.

From here you could either put another seven inch tube down from the clip in the centerpiece of the rig or use a trailer. The fifth tube will add to the impression of a small, tightly packed school of bait swimming along for protection. However, this strategy tends to produce mainly school fish. If you want bigger fish, a better bet is the trailer.

Trailer is the name of a slightly longer tube that rides behind the other tubes on the rig. The idea (hopefully) is to give the look of a larger bait chasing smaller stuff. The larger lure out back gives jumbo fish something to aim at, instead of trying to rush into a small school of small bait. To set up a trailer, clip a black barrel swivel on the rig's centerpiece. Tie a two-foot length of forty pound leader material onto the other eye of the swivel. Onto the other end of the leader, tie a surge hook with a nine inch piece of tubing on it. The larger size of the trailer tube will put you into bigger bass.

The last step in preparing the rig is to put a black Coastlock snap swivel into the front eye of the centerpiece. The pointed end of this type snap keeps the rig from moving side-to-side in the water; thus reducing the chances of "cartwheeling"—a rig spinning wildly in the water instead of running on a steady track.

That's the steps for rigging tubes; now let's look at fishing one of these rigs. Because the mini rig is not as heavy as bigger varieties, you will probably have to put out a bit more wire than you're accustomed to fishing—especially on a running tide. On the other side of the coin, since the rig is lighter, it is good when you turn the boat and drop the lure down on a piece of structure. The lighter rig won't sink as fast; thus reducing the chances of its fouling in the bottom. The small rig is also very useful for fishing in very shallow water—say if the fish are laying in tight to a beach. At those times, you might need only a very short shot of wire or maybe you can take fish with plain mono.

On the negative side, the five tubes of the mini rig are not as "eye-catching" to the fish, so you have to be right on the money with regards to amount of wire and speed of the boat. You have to get the small rig closer to some fish to get them to see it. Bass and blues will see a bigger rig with all its spinning tubes much quicker. However, like I said before, those big rigs are a pain in the donkey to store and fish.

Traces of winter are liable to be with us somewhat longer. If you are eyeing the tackle once more, perhaps you might consider making up a couple of these rigs. The ease with which they fish and amount of space they take up, just might change your mind about umbrella rigs.

One thing you must consider. When the fish are feeding on sand eels, the rigs are the best thing to peddle. There have been plenty of tides in waters all along our coast where the rig was THE method. If you didn't have one in the water, you didn't "catch." Rather than do without, try the best of both worlds: a compact, fish-catchin' umbrella rig.

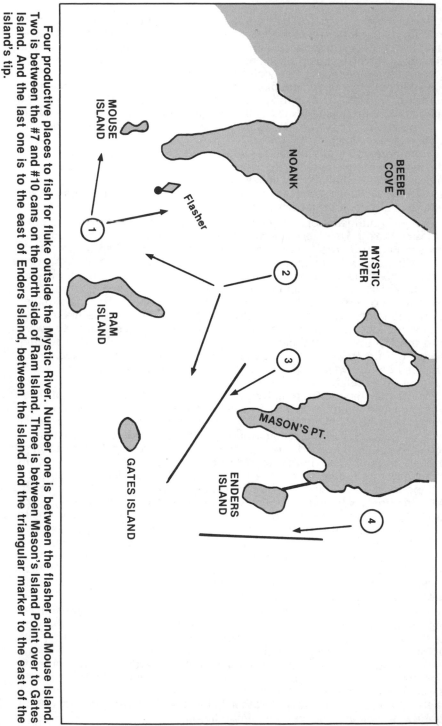

Four productive places to fish for fluke outside the Mystic River. Number one is between the flasher and Mouse Island. Two is between the #7 and #10 cans on the north side of Ram Island. Three is between Mason's Island Point over to Gates Island. And the last one is to the east of Enders Island, between the island and the triangular marker to the east of the island's tip.

MOUSE ISLAND

Flasher

NOANK

BEEBE COVE

MYSTIC RIVER

RAM ISLAND

MASON'S PT.

GATES ISLAND

ENDERS ISLAND

CHAPTER 15

Mystic River Fluke

Looking for a spot to catch a few nice fluke? There are a lot of places that might fill the bill, but how many are within a short drive of a lot of readers?

One of my jobs with *The Fisherman* was doing the Connecticut fishing reports. When a certain spot keeps producing sooner or later even I begin to take note. Such a place, with regard to bigger fluke, is the case with locations in and around Mystic River.

In the course of checking out info for this story, I met with Mr. Albert Erickson of Groton. Mr. Erickson fishes every morning and thus seemed a good man to listen to. He goes mainly to the east and southeast of Enders Island. His favorite drift is between the island and the triangular marker located to the east of the island's tip. There is a deeper section of soft bottom here that holds nice fish. Three years ago, his best was an eighteen pounder; his best trip so far this season has been fourteen fish to eight-and-a-quarter pounds.

As with a lot of fluke fishermen in this area, he uses big smelt for bait. He hooks them once through the head, then brings the hook out and runs it down through the midsection a second time. Incoming is his favorite tide and an east wind produces fluke better than others. However, he has taken his share of fish on other winds. The best time—and only time—for Mr. Erickson is from daybreak to sometime before noon.

If he doesn't get any fish in his number one spot, he will try drifting from the tip of Enders Island over toward the #5 can by Ellis Reef. The deeper water in a line drawn from the island to the can sometimes yields nice fluke.

While I was talking to Mr. Erickson, one Luciano Bellastrini, otherwise known as Flip, was on hand. Flip is a good fluke fisherman and couldn't help being drawn into a conversation about one of his favorite subjects.

Two of Flip's favorite fluke holes are between the flasher at the mouth of the river down to Mouse Island. Another of his spots is between the #7 and #10 cans on the north side of Ram Island. This stretch is part of the east channel out of the river leading between Ram and Mason's Islands out into Fisher's Island Sound.

Flip mentioned the fluke now are full of eggs. Already he's noticed one to two inch fluke in the shallow flats nearby. On the other side of the scale, Flip mentioned reading a book that had a passage about Captain Foster taking a twenty-six pound fluke off Ram Island back in the 1800s. One of the biggest fluke ever to come into Shaffer's Boat Livery, located on the river, was a nineteen pounder caught ten years ago. It seems safe to say the river has a history of bigger fluke. Just as I left to go put this on paper, Flip jokingly told me to hold space on the front cover for the fourteen pounder he was going to catch.

"Patrick" and I made trips here for fluke, just to keep the place honest. We found fish between the tip of Mason's Island back out to Gate's Island. The first part of the trip I went by myself. The fluke were lying in shallow depressions in twenty to twenty-three feet of water. Each time I'd get my ranges down pat, I'd either take fish between two and four-and-a-half pounds or yank the bait away from one before he had a chance to eat it properly.

The next time out, "Patrick" took a fish about four-and-a-half pounds the first drift we made past the tip of Mason's Island. We were drifting on the same ranges as the previous day, only this time the tide was dropping. Unfortunately, fog rolled in, so for the next three hours we fished mainly by guesstimation and compass; never really sure if we were on the money.

As we drifted around in the fog, we started experimenting with small white bucktails laced with a squid strip. The fluke liked them, as did the multitude of squid in the area. At times, the squid hit the fluttering bucktail combo as it made its way to bottom. The squid hits were so numerous you often would set-up too soon when a fluke did grab the lure. With the squid strip on the bucktail, you could actually give the fluke a little line. Fluke will often grab the end of the strip—they eat their way to the hook. The free-spooling gives the fish time to get the bait down inside his mouth. We had many more hits on the bucktail than with the bait just drifted slowly along the bottom on a second rod.

Since these are calm, protected waters, this fishing is well within the range of a fellow with a trailered fourteen footer. There are public launch ramps at Barn Island in the Town of Stonington or Bayberry Lane, Groton (right next to Spicer's). Who knows—maybe we'll be putting your picture on the cover when YOU get to the fourteen pounder ahead of Flip.

We found fish between the tip of Mason's Island back out to Gates Island. This particular trip the fluke were lying in shallow depressions in 20 to 23 feet of water.

Flounderin' Around

Before the fishing gear begins its winter hibernation in attics, cellars or trunks of cars, a lot of shore fishermen go one more round, only this time with winter flounder instead of bass or blues. Flatfish may not cause a hernia when you lift one but catching them consistently requires—as does all types of fishing—effort and thought.

First suggestion we offer is acquiring the services of a chum pot. A chum pot is a wire-mesh, cylindrical cage into which you put ground-up mussels, cat or dog food, whole kernel corn or rice and lots of unorthodox concoctions that ooze out of the pot when it's raised and lowered on the bottom. Most tackle shops have chum pots for sale or you can make your own.

Since a shore fisherman can't move from spot to spot so easily, attracting the fish to his location is important to raising the number of fish you delegate to your wife or girlfriend to clean. A lot of shore fishermen we've witnessed tossed out their rigs, put their rods in a sand spike, then sat back to await the flounders doing all the work. This method produces an occasional flounder on most days and perhaps a couple memory-making trips each fall, but for consistently higher scores you have to work harder than the average fisherman; you have to use a chum pot.

A pot dispensing goodies downstream perks the flounder interest on most days; on some days nothing works except trying again tomorrow. Flounders in the area downstream from a pot move uptide seeking the source of the feed. Once found, they congregate in the area much to an

Sometimes the end of the dock is not always the best. If commercial boats continually throw their gury and racks in one spot, that may be the place holding the most flounders.

angler's delight. In any type of fishing, chumming will outproduce just plain still fishing. Flounder fishing is no exception.

Instead of the standard 1/8" rope that comes with mass-produced pots, some fellows are substituting the same length of 100-300 pound test mono. The mono has less water resistance than the rope so the pot stays in one general spot in the face of stiff currents much better. If the pot won't stay put even with the mono, put in a couple 8 to 12 ounce sinkers prior to filling it with chum.

One of the best situations a shore fisherman can look for to effectively fish with a chum pot is a casting position where the water flows underneath him instead of past him. The perfect example of such a place is a bridge. An angler lowers his chum pot to the bottom on a moving tide, casts his rig in the same general vicinity, starts chumming and hopefully will soon have flats going home to momma via a flounder rig fished close to a chum pot.

A shore fisherman taking a position where the current sweeps past him can't effectively use a chum pot. Number one, he probably has to cast out to the deep water which isn't directly below him as in the case of a bridge. Number two, a shore angler can't raise and lower a pot that has to be thrown out on an angle away from him. Every time he works the pot, he only succeeds in moving the pot right back to him, hence away from his baited rig on the bottom.

However, this doesn't mean an angler in such a position can't use his head and stir up a little activity. We once observed two youthful anglers casting out into a deep hole is a spot where the current swept by, not under their position. The pair had their rigs lying in a deep hole adjacent to a drop-off bordering a shallow flat. The two were fishing in a rather narrow, mud-bottom tidal creek.

One of the two took a grappling hook, went a short distance up-tide and threw the hook out to the flat close to the dropoff and spot where their bait rigs lay on the bottom. Once the hook was on the bottom one youth heaved and hauled on the line causing the hook to gouge out the bottom on its way back to shore. As the hook did so, numerous particles and other matter lying on the bottom were dislodged. This "chum" washed downstream over the dropoff. The fellow on the grappling hook told me it sometimes took as much as one hour before flats took notice but results were usually noticeably better than other anglers out seeking a late-season catch from that same creek.

Even though the pair just mentioned caught fish we still feel a position above a moving current is superior and much less effort with regard to chumming than one alongside a current.

In a lot of tidal waters—rivers and creeks especially—a moving tide stirs up a lot of weed. If an angler's line is strung out across the current then he or she is apt to collect more weeds per time the line is in the water than the angler fishing straight up and down, simply because the former has more line exposed to the flow of the current.

Also, because the length of line is broadside to the current, a heavier sinker is needed. The heavier a sinker, the less the lowly, lightweight flat will fight. The less fight, the less enjoyment a person has fishing. And that's what it's all about.

If you still must fish alongside a current we offer these suggestions. One of the best spots is an inlet. An inlet is any place one body of water flows into another, and this needn't be on a large scale like Charlestown Breachway or the mouth of a large river. An inlet could be the entrance of a tidal creek into a pool or into a larger river or anyplace a moving current is

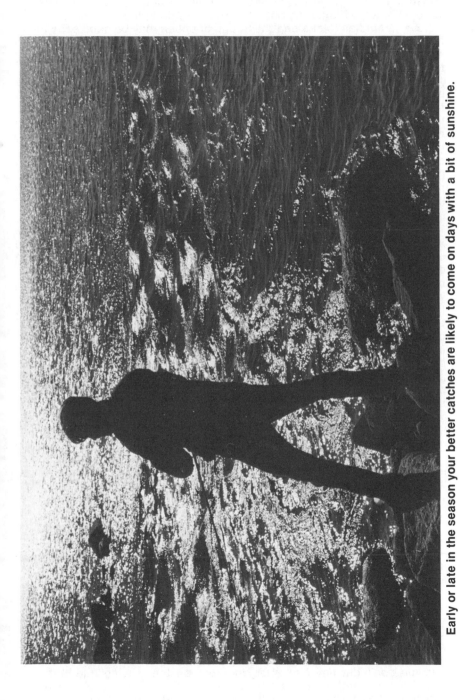

Early or late in the season your better catches are likely to come on days with a bit of sunshine.

forced through a constricted opening forming a tide rip. In such spots the current usually stirs up the bottom, attracting flounders.

Bear in mind an inlet along the Sound or ocean may be good early in the fall but as time wears on the flats will move into the tidal pond or river to spend the winter. The timing of this move depends on the drop in water temperature.

Another favorite of shore anglers is a cove. Most times shallower coves produce during the top of the incoming tide when there's enough water for a flatfish to move up onto the mud flats of a cove to feed. As the tide drops, flounders usually move off the flats back to the deeper water of the nearby channel.

If you caught fish in a cove during high tide but action in the cove slacked off as the tide dropped, maybe you should locate a point of land jutting out into a channel where flats are still feeding in the deeper water of the last part of the tide. Remember a channel lies between the green buoys and the black cans. If you can reach this area from a certain jutting point, this might be a spot to try when the shallow cove literally goes dry.

For our money though we'll take straight up and down positioning. Another good location for above-the-current flatfishing is a dock. We've observed lots of anglers who seem to think the only productive spot on a dock is the very end. "Tain't always so, especially if a commercial fishing boat ties up at the dock." At the end of a commercial man's day, a lot of unwanted fish guts, etc. probably gets dumped over the side. Over a period of time this spot becomes rich with decomposing flesh adding nutrients into the water. This in turn draws flounders to the spot. If the commercial boat consistently ties up in the middle of the dock then the best flounder fishing is liable to be right there in the middle. Conversely, the tide might drop down so much there's not enough water around the middle but it's still possible to get fish out near the end. There's no really pat rule, you just have to put in your time and pay attention to what you're doing and your surroundings.

Let's say you're interested in going flounder fishing. The lighter you go the more fun you'll have. Flounder won't put up much of a tussle on rods meant to remove blues from 120 feet of water in a four knot current. Bank sinkers from one to four ounces should hold in most inshore flounder spots. Hook-wise get some number eight Chestertowns. To construct a simple flounder rig turn to the book *Fishing for Flounder* by Dr. William A. Muller. The diagram there will explain things better than any words set down here.

Next step is rearranging your work schedule so you can get out on warm, sunny days rather than cold, dreary ones. Not only do flounders bite better on such days at this time of year, but you'll enjoy your trip that much more. Plan to be at your spot, not enroute or just heading out to the car, when the tide is one hour past slack water. This insures a fully-moving tide when you arrive.

Once there, bait up your hooks and the pot. Lower both to the bottom, which I hope is directly below you. Tie the end of the pot line to something stationary on the bridge or dock. Start raising and lowering the pot right away so all the juices, etc. will ooze out. Depending on the day it might take up to one hour to get flats concentrated where you want them right after you drop your line in the water.

If you don't get any fish after one hour on the moving tide quit until another day or come back on the next tide. Sometimes you'll have fast fishing right away but it gradually dies off to a slow pick even though you still have a moving tide and a chum pot in the water. What might happen is all the juices washed out of your chum leaving very little to escape downtide to interest the flounders. If that happens rebait your pot.

Sometimes you'll get fish every time you work the pot. No fooling, we've seen this happen with our own bloodshot baby blues. Every time we raised and lowered the pot a flounder grabbed the bait. If we didn't continually work with the pot, we got nothing except some late-season sunshine.

Continual filling and emptying pots can be messy especially if the procedure is multiplied by lots of anglers using just one particular location on plenty of tides. If the area isn't policed by the anglers themselves, local residents may complain about the smell. If enough people complain, soon there's one less shore fishing spot.

We're done flounderin' for now. We wish you well with our suggestions. They've been set down before you because time and many fishing trips (not just our own) have shown them to be worthy of consideration by the greatest people in the world; the readers of *The Fisherman.*

Flatfish may not cause a hernia when you lift some but catching them consistently requires thought and effort.

Author with cod of 50, 50½ and 42 lbs. taken during one very productive day with jigs out off Block Island.

CHAPTER 17

The Iron Clams

Richie threw the jig toward the Montauk headboat. It sank amongst the 8" sand eels in hopes of the first fish of the morning. Crowds were light that weekday. He had plenty of elbow room to set the hook right after a 30 lber. grabbed the lure before it hit bottom. Chalk up another victim of an iron clam.

The last time I heard that expression was at the end of a polite verbal battle. That Wednesday a fellow from the Connecticut heartland berated another for thinking he could catch cod with jigs. All the way out, intertwined with other bits of hot air, he displayed his knowledge.

The first stop gave up some small fish—all with bait. Zip for the jiggers. On the 20 minute ride further out the bait dunker smiled broadly, having proved his point. Contrary to some opinions, though, there is justice in this world. On the next drop, the first fish to come up was 51½ lbs. with a jig firmly attached to his jaw. That was followed by a 25 lb. pollack supplied by Richie. Soon after, a 51 lber. was placed in the white fish box. All the commotion did not go unnoticed in the wheelhouse. Even the gray-haired gentleman with the horn-rimmed glasses started jigging. He watched as Richie put down his rod to gaff a 42 lber. At this point, an elderly man from Waterbury said, loud enough for Hot Air to hear, "Looks like they're taking the iron clams today."

Call them what you will when you will, the use of jigs on the Block Island grounds is usually effective in April. Find a batch of sand eels and more than likely you've found fish. The day after the preceding paragraph's trip, Captain George Lockhart took his first 50 lber. of the year, also with a jig. That was April 23, 1981.

Over the last couple seasons, our reports section carried notice of this action. Last year by mid-month we wrote of Tom Phillips of Willimantic with a couple hangers. On the 20th, Chet Butnik of Hartford had ten fish to further add fuel to the fire. That week was good. It peaked with fish all over the boats on the 23rd. The year before was much of the same. We had reports off and on from the 6th through the end of the month. One very productive day in 1980 was April 17th. The usual start of this fishing is somewhere around Easter.

Along with reports, we've also tried to tell people that jigs do have their place in the yearly scheme of things. When cod are on baitfish, especially sand eels, jigs usually outfish clams. Each April sees fishermen board boats with only bait rigs. They come unprepared.

While there are lots of jigs on the market, the two most popular types are the A series and the Norway jigs. The A series was first introduced by Ava Tackle Company. Their product was broader than the standard four-sided diamond. As such, it has more action. This jig is best used with the squidding method. You drop the lure to the bottom, then take five to ten slow turns. If there's no hit, take the reel out of gear and repeat the procedure.

Squidding is popular with a lot of the Montaukers and people who don't like the up and down effort of using a Norway jig. This can be tiring over a five to six hour period to those unaccustomed to the exertion.

After Ava, other companies came out with their versions of an A series jig such as S&G Lures in Brooklyn, New York. Bridgeport offered something similar with an even broader model called the Slab Jig. All these lures will catch codfish. A friend of mine did well fishing the North Rip in a private boat last spring with a 30 lb. graphite outfit, 20 lb. line and a 4 oz. Slab jig. He slowly squidded the lure off the bottom as the boat drifted back to the rip. Never did he have any big fish but on some mornings the totals reached the teens with top fish of 12 lbs. All the catching was over by ten, which gave him time to run back to Watch Hill, get some sleep and still make the second shift at Harris.

The A series type jigs are NOT the best ones to use with up and down sweeps of the rod. This technique is best left to the traditional, fluted Norway jig with treble hooks. You use this jig by dropping it to the bottom, then with sweeps of the rod, keep it moving up and down within 5' or so of the bottom. It's more work than squidding, but will keep the lure closer to the bottom more of the time.

Some days, when cod are feeding on crabs, are tough for jiggers. The fish have their noses pointed down, not up the other way when they chase the eels. On those trips even a slowly-squidded jig is—most of the time—exiting their line of sight. A slowly worked Norway jig is right down where they are eating. Because it stays closer to the bottom longer, it's more apt to be seen. Please keep in mind this is not always the case. At times the only alternative is to switch to bait.

Last April 25th we picked slowly at the fish in the morning. By midday, however, bait was taking nice fish. Jigs were coming out a distant second until a couple of us greatly reduced the jigging motion. We didn't keep up with the bait nor did we kill 'em. We did get some fish to eat a jig.

The standard weight of the A series jigs used around Block Island is 6 to 8 oz. I've weighed some mass produced jigs in this category that were supposed to weigh 8 oz., yet turned out to be 6½. It's probably only a small point, but it doesn't seem quite fair. If you are going to pay for an 8 oz. jig, you should get an 8 oz.

The weights used most often for Norway jigs are 8 to 12 oz. There's usually not much need to go heavier. Since the tackle used in Rhode Island is lighter than that up north, you will have to work very hard moving a 16 or 17 oz. lure through the water. For all the extra effort, I doubt you'll get any more fish.

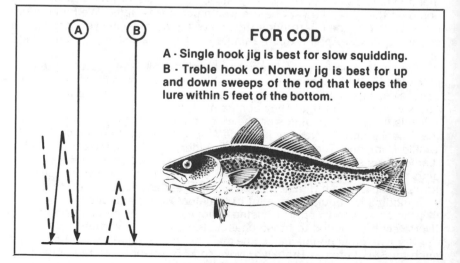

FOR COD

A - Single hook jig is best for slow squidding.
B - Treble hook or Norway jig is best for up and down sweeps of the rod that keeps the lure within 5 feet of the bottom.

While April is a good time around Block Island, it's not the only month you can do well. For instance, in May the Gail Frances made a 5,000 lb. haul offshore. Top fish was 61 lbs. with good numbers of 40s. In the same time period a friend of mine watched the Messalina pull into the dock with a cockpit full of fish. Other charter and private boats also did well.

Since we've told you the good points, we'll also mention some of the not-so-good trips. A couple years ago in April several of us took one cod apiece and a dozen or so ocean pout. Not much jigging that day. Last April 24th we picked a fair amount in the morning, but never had a sniff past 11 a.m. On April 29th we struggled unproductively against southwest winds better than 25 mph; the whole while the wind howled, the weather forecast still gave 10 to 15. Around noon the tide changed, the wind backed off and George Lockhart called us over. We fished fast for an hour trying to make up for lost time.

Any number of boats await your decision to fish. If it's blowing too much for your own rig, consider one of the bigger boats. Whatever route you decide, go fishing. April is a good one for iron clams out by Block Island.

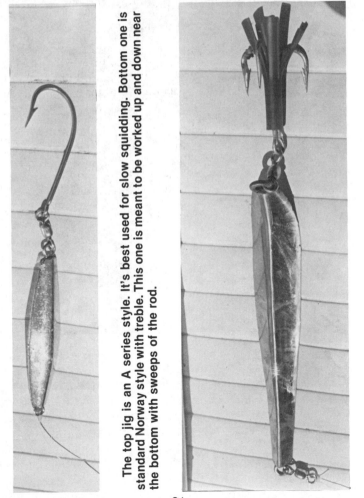

The top jig is an A series style. It's best used for slow squidding. Bottom one is standard Norway style with treble. This one is meant to be worked up and down near the bottom with sweeps of the rod.

One trick that may or may not work for you is the addition of a small, plastic squid above the hook on a bait rig.

CHAPTER 18

Thinking About Cod

The fellow across the aisle from our booth at the fishing show was a diehard blue water fisherman. During the season he captains a 31 foot Rampage, fishing at times off the Vineyard, at times south of Point Judith from the inside fleet all the way south of the Fishtail. The guy loves offshore, but come the spring he starts thinking about cod.

While we were impressed with the man's store of knowledge, we were also interested to hear he likes groundfishing on occasion. Such, I suspect, is the way of a lot of readers right now. They may chase white marlin in the summer, but once the boat gets in or the days get longer, they'll head out in their own boat or buy a ride on a charter or party vessel for the fun and fillet of codfishing.

Fishermen are forever tinkerers, looking for that little touch that will give them a few more fish in the box or perhaps the edge over the guy next door. Each year we fish we see a few new wrinkles that add to the store of knowledge. Last season was no exception. During one June trip to wrecks south of Block Island, I saw a couple party boat captains from Sheepshead Bay, New York on board. They fished with the standard bait rig but added a small rubber skirt over the hook. By day's end they not only caught more fish but one won the pool with a 44 pounder.

On the ride home I spoke with the captain about the trick just witnessed. He said the skirts on bait rigs weren't new, just a wrinkle not seen in the last several years. Later in the year the two New Yorkers again visited southern New England and again caught well using skirts draped over a hook wetted with a piece of clam.

As time ticks by we're hearing more stories from bottom fishermen who have had success using small light sticks. These are miniature versions of the lights used by night by longline and rod and reel swordfishermen to catch broadbills along the canyon walls. Smaller versions have been on the market the last couple seasons. They give off light without heat and can be attached to a leader in a variety of ways. The ones I've seen have suggestions for doing such right on the back of the package. Those are made by the American Cyanamide Company and sold under the name Lunker Lights. Some of the people who have volunteered information don't want their names used in print, but we can wonder aloud if readers in northern New England who bait fish in deep water for haddock might not give these light sticks a try.

Speaking of haddock, a couple subscribers came by our booth at the Boston Boat Show to voice their opinion that one cannot catch a haddock on a jig. Bait will do better by you, but you can jig some haddock, including some real nice ones. Our two best are twin 16 pounders, both caught with jigs. One came from a deeper edge on a Cashes trip; the other from the 190 hill off Kennebunkport, Maine. The biggest haddock I ever saw in the flesh was a 19 lb. 15 oz. giant jigged up in 260 feet of water on the edge of Great South Channel by veteran codfisherman Dick Lincoln. In all three of these cases, the key was a slower jig stroke with a particularly watchful eye as the jig went slowly back down.

Another couple readers stopped by the booth in Boston to inquire about addresses for getting some of the leadheads we've written about in earlier issues. These lures are not taking the codfish world by storm, but a few people are trying them. Up here in Yankeeland, that's about the best you can hope for. Any reader interested can write to: Mr. Rich Andrus, 708 E. Main, Millville, NJ 08332, or Mr. Fred Vander Werff, Sebastes Fishery Company, Box 310, Kirkland, WA 98033. Both companies make these lures in different sizes and styles.

We can tell you we had good luck with leadheads on the '86 Georges trips but poor to moderate results on the wrecks off the southern New England coast. We did see Mr. Joe Stella take a 45 lb. hake on a leadhead spiced up with a piece of clam from a wreck south of Martha's Vineyard.

Leadheads also worked well on a trip out of Wychmere Harbor, fishing off Chatham on the Sue Z with Captain Joe Zottolli. Three of us caught a fair load including a 35 pounder that grabbed a leadhead fished with light rod and 16 pound line.

Just after we spoke with the two readers about using leadheads and curly tailed plastic worms, we saw Captain Les Showm of the Rosey S coming down the aisle. During the summer months Les takes bluefish charters, but during the spring, fall and winter, he fishes commercially for cod on the grounds east and southeast of Monomoy. It's interesting to note he used to use the standard 180 pound mono and handline, but since switched to rod and reel because that's catching better. His favorite teaser above the jig is now a Red Gill which is getting more fish than a tube. We might also add he was right in the middle of a bite of market fish last April when a 186 lb. halibut grabbed hold.

I asked Les about using leadheads, but he said the fish would keep tearing off the plastic worm, so he'd have to stop and thread another one up the shank of the lure. We've had the same "problem" on a few Georges Banks trips, but were ready to go back into the cabin for another worm. One white, plastic wriggler accounted for 24 cod before number 25 bit the tail clean off. To keep the worms tight on the shank of the leadhead we borrowed an idea from freshwater fisherman, Rod Teehan. Rod uses a drop of Crazy Glue to keep black, 9 inch rubber worms on the shank of his ¼ ounce lures; so we did the same with our 12 ounce bugs.

Speaking of freshwater, we are always poking through freshwater mags looking for some tidbit that might lend a hand with saltwater fishing. From time to time, we've read about the countdown system for fishing sinking plugs over some type structure. Last May we got a chance to put some of that bass busting info to work. We were anchored on the big wreck south of Nantucket with 6 to 20 lb. pollock for the taking. As the boat swung tight on the anchor, we found ourselves right atop the mammoth liner. The trick was cast as far uptide as possible, then count as the jig first hit bottom. If it took, say a count of 15 to hit the wreck, you stopped the lure on the next toss at 13 or 14. That way you were right in the pollock's front yard without fear of snagging, something plaguing a lot of people on board.

Also in the freshwater articles are numerous accounts of bass fishing after dark. The thought might then go to codfish after dark. We can tell you about a big party boat that fished Georges Bank last season that had some fish in the 40s on bait at night. The captain anchored the boat over a wreck close to Great South Channel. Once the tide stopped running people who didn't mind losing sleep got up to fish clams for some steakers which won pools.

On one of our July Georges trips last year, we had some excellent after dark fishing one evening when slack water coincided with dusk. From 8:30 to sometime after 10, cod from 10 to 20 lbs. steadily grabbed jigs and tubes until the tide started to run to the north, at which time the bite petered out. I wonder, though, if cod get going on a good afternoon bite if people couldn't stick around into the night to pick up a couple more?

A groundfish that seems to bite well at night is silver hake, called blue hake up in the Gulf of Maine. On one of our first trips to the now famous big wreck south of Nantucket, we had banner pollock fishing as the sun set. Once it went down, we swung off the wreck and switched over to 12 oz. jigs to catch silver hake up to 50 lbs. with the same up and down motion associated with codfishing. We caught hake until our arms tired, so it wasn't just a couple oddballs. One veteran skipper later said he never heard of hake on lures, let alone such numbers. It's interesting to note we couldn't catch hake on jigs in the daylight, but they hit them readily once the sun went down. In one case, two free swimming hake followed a hooked buddy all the way up from 240 feet down. You could see the two swimming around In the boat lights as the third member of their party was gaffed and added to the growing pile.

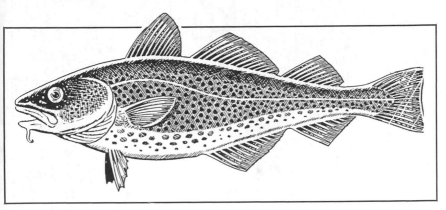

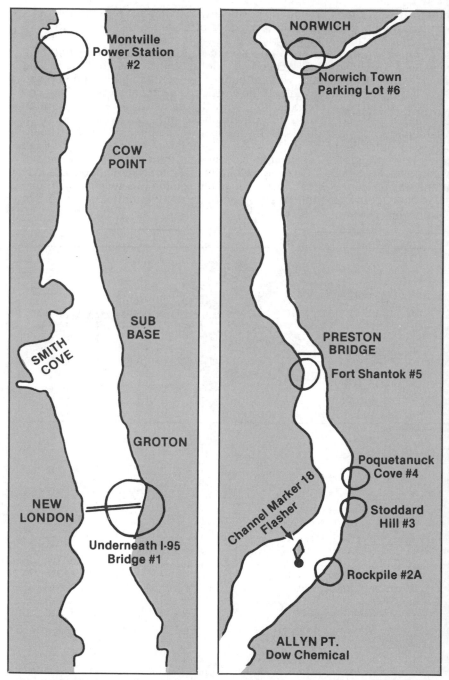

Moving up river, some of the more popular shorefishing locations—with access—are underneath the I-95 bridge #1, Montville Power House #2, the Rockpile #2A, Stoddard Hill #3, Poquetanuck Cove, #4, Fort Shantok #5 and Norwich Town parking lot #6.

CHAPTER 19

Thames River Bass Spots

Editor's Note: Over the last few years laws governing the river have changed considerably. Anglers are now aware of strict size, bag and seasonal limits. Please make sure you consult state regulations or if you're in doubt, we suggest you call the State DEP.

Over the last couple weeks, we ran a series of articles on blackfish spots in eastern Long Island Sound. We had such good response on this type of article that we will present more, starting with this story on the Thames River.

It was researched from back issues, stories, talks with tackle dealers and most important—personal experience. Please keep in mind this is by no means a complete list of places to fish from shore. They are, however, spots with access. A lot of the other places along the river require either a boat to get to them, or you have to cross private property. That isn't an insurmountable obstacle. A person can get permission to cross somebody's land, but we can't publicize these places. The following selection, though, should get a person interested in the bass fishery some place to start.

We start up around Norwich. The town parking lot, on an outgoing tide, is the scene of people gathered to cast plugs, not go shopping. For several years we've carried reports of good fishing here anywhere from the middle to end of November. The first prolonged cold snap of the late fall seems to start the fishing, though this seems to be just a general rule of thumb. To reach here, go up Route 12 on the east side of the river. Once you get to the bridge in town, take the Route 169 turnoff. Go two or three blocks, take a left to double back along the river to the lot. This location is marked #6 on the accompanying charts.

Next stop is marked #5. This is Fort Shantok, a very, very popular place for fellows dunking blood or sand worms on the bottom. Many, many nights, a row of lanterns can be observed by one fishing the less crowded shore on the other side. A couple people I once spoke to from both the Hartford Surf Club and Long Cove Landing said they've done well at times using live mummies as a bass bait. Make sure you use a float to keep the bait off the bottom. Access to Fort Shantok is along the west side of the river. Take Route 2A, heading north, then watch for the sign on the right-hand side of the road to Ft. Shantok. Follow this road all the way down till you see a second sign (on the left-hand side of the road). Take a left there, following the road through the Park until you reach the parking lot. The river will be in front of you and most of the baitfishing is done to the south.

Going down river from Fort Shantok, we come to the RR bridge across the entrance of Poquetanock Cove (marked #4) into the river. On an outgoing tide a person can cast a plug or a small bucktail into the low of tide out into the river. On several different nights over the last three years, I've fished from shore here while a boat was anchored further out in the current, near the dropoff of the river channel. The freshwater coming out of the cove is usually a bit warmer than that of the river. Also it carries bait with it.

Number three is the stretch just up the river from the parking lot at Stoddard Hill Park. Take Route 12, then watch for the sign for the park entrance. Fishermen don't seem to be bothered here after dark. As you walk along the river from the lot you'll see a wall along the river's edge. There will be a cleared stretch with remnants of fires and probably, and unfortunately, the litter that always accumulates where people fish. This is a spot to dunk bait that's not near as crowded as Fort Shantok.

The rock pile is the nickname for spot 2A. For a shorecaster, this is just opposite the pile of rocks supporting a blinker, designated channel marker 18. On the east side of the river the channel bends in close, well within the cast of the average rod. In better days of bassfishing we've carried reports of 40 lb. bass caught from this stretch. Access is off Route 12 just beyond Stoddard Park. There's a foot path available on close inspection.

Next to last locale is the Montville Power House, labeled #2. When the plant is pumping, hot water flows out into a cove, then the river itself. The hot water creates an artificial environment for the wintering bass. For instance, last year on November 18th, the water temp here was 64°. The same night it was 45° at Poquetanock and a chilly 43° at Fort Shantok.

To reach the power house, take Route 32 to Uncasville. Take Power House Road to the end. Take a right, then your first left. As you go into the plant, you'll see a dirt lot off to the left. More than likely there will be other cars parked there. Get out, walk along the RR tracks until you come to a small trestle. Start casting lures right around the top of the tide from the trestle on down to the first clump of trees. Baitfishermen always congregate down by the trees, rather than close to the trestle. Fellows in small boats fish the stream of hot water right where it exits the plant. That spot, though, is off limits to the average shore fisherman.

Last spot for this story is under the twin bridges of I-95. People, I'm sure, will have no trouble finding this landmark. People fish both the west and east bank under the bridges. One thing you might try is taking two rods with you. Use one on the bottom with worms; with the other, try casting a weighted 5½" Rebel or RedFin, a 52MII Mirrolure or ¼ or ½ oz. bucktail; try spicing it up with a small piece of worm. Work the lures slower than normal as the cold water slows down the bass's metabolism.

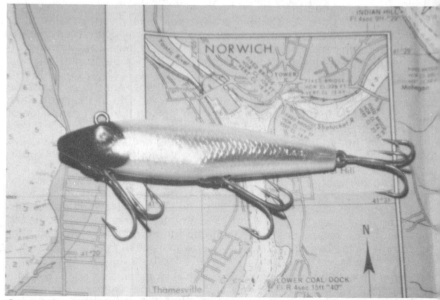

One of the most popular plugs for Thames bassfishing is the 52MII Mirrolure.

CHAPTER 20

Light Tackle Blackfishing

Over the last couple years we've tried to alert readers to the exciting possibilities about light tackle in saltwater. This needn't be reserved for people with big sportfishermen, rather it can be for the surf caster or in the case of this article, the fellow who likes bottom fishing.

In a recent reader survey (results will be printed in an upcoming issue), we found that 40 percent of our audience fishes both fresh and ocean. If you are one of those types, might we suggest toting some of your light rods down to the Sound or ocean the next time you go tautog fishing. An eight pound largemouth on a worm rod is fine, but there's many, many more eight pound blackfish around. And, wait until the 'tog eats the wrong crab and heads for home. You'll see how far the rod will bend.

Spinning or baitcasting will do the job. I've got a small Shimano baitcaster rated for 1/4 to 5/8 ounce lures. This rod, though, will handle sinkers to two ounces without undue strain. Remember you are not casting this weight, just dropping it over the side. I also am fortunate to own a beauty of a Fenwick ultralight boron spin stick rated for 1/16 to 1/4 ounce stuff. That, too, can be used with tiny sinkers when the tide permits.

The tide or lack of it is the key to fishing light. You can have one or two such outfits aboard, but if the current is whistling you won't be able to use them until it stops or slows down. For instance, with my two little rods you could fish the reefs on the oceanside of Fisher's Island with the Shimano conventional about two hours before slack water unless it's an exceptional day. Even in 30 to 35 feet of water, the two ounce sinker keeps the ten pound line handy to the bottom. Sometime just before slack, I bring out the little spinner and use it with 1/4 ounce sinkers. With that rod, though, it's better to be in shallower water, say 25 feet or less, since you don't have much hook setting power.

Ever caught a four pound tautog on four pound line with rods meant for hatchery trout or calico bass? Better hang on and make sure your sneakers are laced all the way up. If not, your partner is liable to hear a splash and mention it's kind of late in the season for swimming. Once you set the hook the little rods go over like the Ugly Stik ads and stay that way. The blackfish takes off like a school bass with you trying to keep him out of his front yard. That's the fun of the whole operation.

Everyone seems to favor a different rigging for blacks. The fellow who taught me said to keep things simple: the less hardware, the better. At the time we used stiff boat rods with 50 lb. Ande mono which could probably double for barge towing. My instructor tied a loop in the end of his line, then a dropper knot about ten inches up from that. A sinker went in the end loop and a snelled blackfish hook in the dropper knot. It was simple, neat and effective.

With the four or ten pound line you can't follow suit as the line would break soon after you hooked your first fish. What you might try is get some small three-way swivels, snelled hooks of your choice, a spool of 30 pound mono and some sinkers. First step is to take your running line and double it over with the help of a Spider Hitch knot. That's a very common knot detailed in most books or pamphlets on knot tying. For safety's sake, you want about six feet or so, especially the four pound, doubled over. Take the

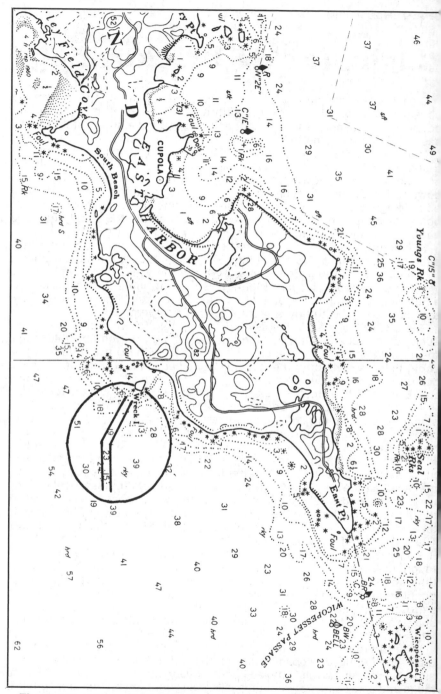

There are many productive places to fish for tautog in southern New England. One usually good place is the reef to the southeast of Wreck Island on the oceanside of Fisher's Island.

end of that and tie it around one eye of the swivel with a clinch knot. Next step is to loop one of the snelled hooks of your choice in another eye of the swivel. Last step is to take about a 12 inch piece of the 30 pound mono. Tie a loop in one end and tie the other to the last eye of the swivel. Place a sinker in the loop and you are ready to fish.

Some very proficient blackfishermen have different ways to prepare a green crab for bait. My instructor told me a blackfish eats a crab's legs and all when he's feeding, so that's the way a bait should be presented. He'd cut a crab in half and place that section on a hook. He hooked the crab through one of the leg sockets by pushing the hook point from the inside of the crab on out.

One very important point in blackfishing in productive waters is amount of bait. Two to three dozen crabs per angler per tide isn't going overboard on your bait bill. If you get into the right spot those baits will go in short order. You might consider four to five dozen per passenger the next time out. On some hot and hectic trips to Southwest Reef off Westbrook, Ct., I've seen two anglers go through a five gallon pail filled to the brim.

One thing we have here in southern New England is the world's best tautog fishing. There's no directed commercial pressure on a large scale, hence there's millions and millions of them around. And, when you drop a crab down you just never know when a monster will take hold. There are blacks from 15 to 20 to ? pounds around but getting them off the bottom may be another matter. Anyway, readers can fish for tautog anywhere from Stamford, Ct. up through at least Gurnet Point in Plymouth—in season. I've talked with people who saw blacks at the jetties at the mouth of the Merrimac River but whether there's any fishery from, say Boston Harbor on up remains to be seen.

Since Fisher's Island just off Westerly, R.I. is just out my back door, that's where I've done some blackfishing. If you've been checking the reports from Shaffers Boat Livery you'd know Flip has been telling us about a guy from New Britain who's been doing pretty well on the reefs on the ocean or south side of the island.

Under the right conditions you can have a ball using light tackle for blackfish.

There's any number of rocky places to fish from the east end of the island down to Wilderness Point. One usually productive spot is the reef that runs out from Wreck Island in generally a SE direction. The reef is irregular and bends a bit but the high spots are there, usually marked by pot buoys.

If you run over this reef from east to west with your chart machine running, you undoubtedly see the high points. At that point some people might tie up on a pot line or some mark the high spot, then anchor up so the back of their boat is on the peak, or I've seen others who get a little ways down-tide from the top.

If you arrive on the strength of the tide, the little rods will likely wait for an hour, maybe more. On days with strong tides, however, the best fishing might not be until the tide eases, so the little rods come out about the time fishing is picking up.

It's very important to have hook points extra sharp since you don't have much power to set the hook. Even hooks just out of the package could use a touching up with a good file or stone. If you don't you'll just roll fish after fish over, especially if you use a tiny spin rod.

Here's another opportunity to have some more fun with your fishing. You can bet your last green crab you'll be seeing more such stories over the years as we think saltwater fish and little rods are an exciting mix.

CHAPTER 21

New Haven Blues

The train went by about 50 feet away. The bus followed shortly. With the noise gone Bob nodded in the direction of the bridge, saying "The biggest blue I ever saw in my life was caught here!" That day this bridge was littered with fish.

Bob is Bob Swerling from Guilford, the bridge is the Townsend Avenue span in New Haven, and the blue weighed a couple ounces over 20. The bus headed toward East Haven; the train went in the opposite direction and that bridge is the most unlikely looking spot for bluefish I ever saw.

Giant oil tanks to either side; tall office buildings over one shoulder; the I-95 overpass over the other; cars, buses, trains, college girls and other assorted humans whizzing by in their cars 50 feet behind you and underneath the murky Quinnipiac River carries assorted debris, oil slicks and bunker to waiting blues.

Schools of bunker are the reason the blues like the area around the bridge and even further up the river. This year and last hundreds of blues from 8 to 20 pounds grabbed bunker and lures tossed from the southern side of the bridge. Such quantity and quality were the reasons Bob and myself decided to give the bridge a couple shots two weeks ago.

Bob works in a camera shop in New Haven during the day, so we agreed to meet around 6 p.m. at the bridge. When I got there only fishing for snapper blues took place. Two guys down in the corner by the New Haven Oil Terminal used large red and white floats clipped 4 feet ahead of a small metal lure. The rig went about 75 out. Every time the float bounced on retrieve, the lure underneath flashed. Not too many casts did these two come up empty handed.

Out on the center of the bridge other snapper samplers used bait or a ¼ ounce diamond jig. One little boy cast out a bobber, two BB split shot and number six hook with a small shiner up into the incoming tide. The split shot got the bait down into the current quickly. About every third cast a snapper grabbed the bait as the flat passed directly underneath the bridge.

A teenager fished small shiners right on the bottom. He didn't get near as many snappers but he did get some small herring plus a tiny sea robin. A third fisherman cast a diamond jig in the direction of the sand bar in West Haven. As the incoming tide carried his jig back toward the bridge, he jigged the lure. Connection with a snapper occurred every fifth or sixth cast.

For bigger blues, chunks on the bottom got the most play. Later on, some guys chucked out whole bunker threaded on a long shanked 9/0 instead of a chunk on a medium shank 8/0. Two to four ounce sinkers, fish finder rigs and wire leaders completed the rigging. I noticed one follow fishing with whole bunker using Steelon for leader. He went a step beyond everybody else by using double sleeves to secure the leader to both hook and barrel swivel.

Bob arrived as the sun hit the 6 p.m. mark. We shot the breeze as the local crabs made short work of my bunker chunk. About 20 minutes on the bottom was rebait time.

Phil Wetmore once related a similar experience to me. Seems Phil spent one very soggy, lonely night on the rocks underneath the bridge without any fish. As the night wore on, Phil's patience wore out. The final straw was the head of a huge bunker reduced to one eyeball dangling from the hook after only 10 minutes in the water. Remedy for the exasperation was a cup of coffee at the all-night diner a couple of blocks to the west.

Out of a dozen fishermen that night only two tried lures. One fellow put a yellow Goo Goo Eyes Big Daddy (good color choice in the murky water) in the water from down along the rocks. Another fished a two ounce Smilin' Bill with yellow pork rind (yellow side down) from atop the center of the bridge. Neither fisherman got anything. The only fish caught hit a chunk.

As we waited for a hit Bob and I tossed around some ideas if we were to fish the bridge regularly. Chumming on an outgoing tide sure seems a good idea. If four or five guys continually dropped small pieces of bunker into the water any blues in the vicinity should take notice. A chunk fished without a weight and allowed to drift back with the current might fill a sack for somebody some day.

Bluesfishermen in the Providence and Thames Rivers do the blues in nicely with live eels. Ken's Tackle Shop in Groton recently reported having trouble keeping eels in stock thanks to hungry blues underneath the I-95 bridge. On the outgoing tide an eel could be allowed to drift out from the Townsend Bridge then reeled back slowly.

If you plan to fish the bridge regularly, borrow an idea used in the Pro-

Late in the afternoon, an angler wades and casts for blues at the Sandbar, one very popular spot around New Haven.

vidence River. Up there guys take large treble hooks and grind the barbs off. Enough stout cord is tied to the treble to reach the water. When a blue lies beaten below, the treble is lowered, then jigged hard to "gaff" the fish.

Some anglers attach a split ring to the eye of the treble. On to the split ring they add a snap swivel. When the blue is ready for the gaff they clip the snap to their line, letting the treble slide down to the fish.

Nobody needed the gaff much the whole time we stayed on the bridge. Reason for the lack of blues I'm told was all the freshwater runoff from the storm the week of September 26th. Any time such occurrences happen, fishing is lousy until salinity and bunker get re-established.

On the morning of September 26th, in a steady rain, one man got ten blues from the bridge. The next day catches were way down. As of October 2nd most of the blues were out in the harbor along City Point, the sand bar and Savin Rock. The blues didn't have to go up into the river. The bunker were right in the harbor.

Such reasoning made sense to Bob and me. The next couple times out we poked around at the sand bar, behind the Coast Inn and Savin Rock. The beaches in this area are very shallow. You wade on low water an easy 1/4 to 3/8 of a mile out from the Coast Inn before water reaches waist level.

Last year about the end of October Bob and Pete Luto got nice blues after dark this way. They waded out on low tide until the water reached the hole in the crotch of Bob's waders. The pair snagged one of the hundreds of bunker milling around off the Savin Rock piers then live-lined them for blues up to I believe 16 pounds. Bob described the action as some of the most exciting he's ever experienced.

Given some fish in the area I believe an enterprising angler could do the same in the summer at night, only with poppers. I know of a couple hot-shot surfmen fishing at a location a short drive to the east of New Haven who got blues in three to five feet of water. The blues feed in an area completely exposed at low tide. After dark, just after the tide turned the pair waded out to chest level. The more noise the popper made the more blues they caught. Best night was almost 200 pounds of blues between 10 and 16 pounds. I'll bet somebody could do the same somewhere between Savin Rock and the sandbar.

While we didn't do near as good as 200 pounds, some fish were in the area around the sandbar. One evening I met a young fellow who got blues to 11 pounds just before high tide the morning before. This fellow liked his poppers to splash a lot, so he took the swimming plate off a yellow Goo Goo Eyes Husky Dude. The lure cast further without the plate and threw up much more water than the 2¼ ounce Creek Chub Striper Strike I had.

The next morning the water by the sandbar was just about high and crystal clear. The transparent clarity of this water sharply contrasted with that under the Townsend Bridge, a short distance to the north.

Instead of showing on the jetty side, like they did the previous morning, a few blues prowled the northern side. Out of ten guys plugging poppers only two got all the hits and fish. Reason I thought was these two caused the most commotion in the clear water with their plugs. It's been my experience, at least with blues on poppers, the more times you make a plug push water, the less you bring it "silently" through the water, the more blues you'll attract to all the ruckus.

In that plus plenty other instances the effectiveness of a popper directly increased to the number of "pops" per given period. This is the principle behind the pencil popper which is an underrated, underfished lure especially suited for use with a limber spinning rod.

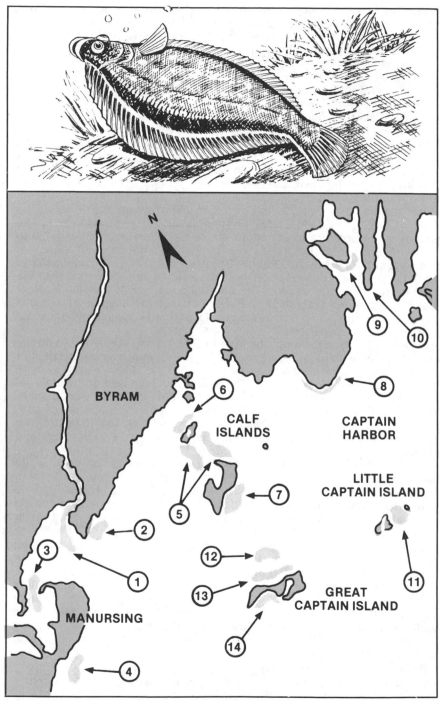

The circles with numbers inside are locations referred to in the story. The lines or circles the arrows point to are the most productive sections.

CHAPTER 22

Greenwich Flounder Locations

For the last 18 years Mr. Eckard Fraude, called Ed by the people who come in his store, has been selling tackle from 242 Water St. in Greenwich. As you might expect, a person there that long builds up a good deal of knowledge about local waters. So when we wanted to do a story about flounder fishing locations here, we turned to the owner of Rudy's Tackle Barn.

One of the best locations earlier in the season is right in the channel of the Byram River. From somewhere around Rudy's, right down to the breakwater at the mouth of the river, one might catch flounder. Most of the fish will be ½ to 1¼ pounds, with the average around ¾ pounds. This is location number one.

If you faced the breakwater from outside the mouth of the river, another worthwhile location would be off to your right. On our chart it's marked number 2. This is Hawthorne Beach. Fish in around the stretch the arrow points to. Off to the left of the river breakwater, behind north Manursing Island, is a sheltered body of water locals call the Mill Pond. There used to be an old grist mill nearby. The "deeper" water between the tip of the island and the shore (the entrance to the pond) is the place to fish. Moving tides are the best with the slowest time so far this year being high slack water. The Mill Pond is number three.

Moving along the sound side of north Manursing Island we'll go outside the number one can at the river mouth. From there we go down the island until we're off the Westchester County Beach Club. At that point, we've arrived at location four. After you've taken stock of this spot, it's off to the east, over around Calf Island. Between Calf and Shell Island is a stretch of flat bottom. On either side of that flat stretch, marked number five, is decent flounder fishing. Plus, you might try to the northwest of Shell Island, number six, or off the southeast side of Calf, number seven. Things always seem easy when you get info from the right person.

Still moving to the east we now find ourselves over around Greenwich Harbor. One can fish around Field Point in a boat or at Grass Island or the pier at the end of Steamboat Road if you like to fish from shore. Those locales are numbers 8, 9 and 10, respectively.

Now it's time to move a bit offshore. You could try the sand bar between Little Captain Island and Island Beach. You'll locate that one by looking for number 11. Our last three selections are number 12, 13 and 14. Twelve is just to the southeast of Cormorant Reef not far from the number one can. Thirteen is on the beach side of Great Captain Island while the last is to the south/southeast of Great Captain at a point where the shore line forms a cove.

That does us for now. What you've just read is really valuable info. Just think how long it would take a newcomer to find out those spots in one sitting. And I wouldn't be surprised if people who've fished here awhile have learned a spot or two. In any event, we hope you've enjoyed the story. If you get a nice mess of flounder, don't thank us; thank the man from Rudy's Tackle Barn.

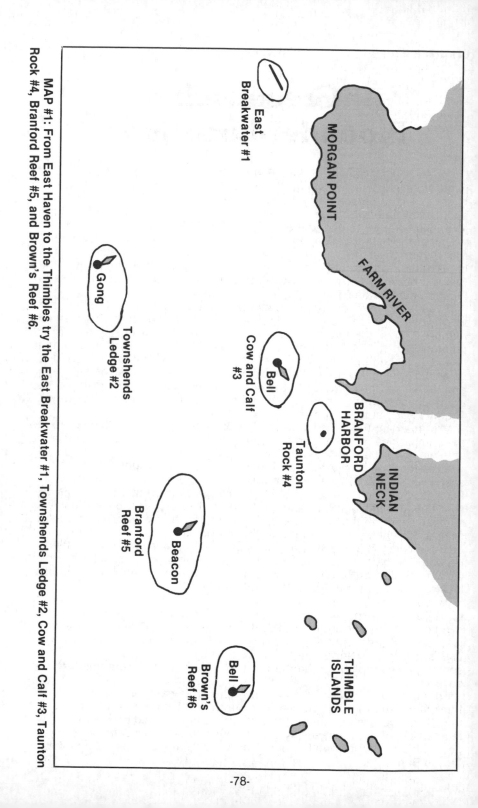

MAP #1: From East Haven to the Thimbles try the East Breakwater #1, Townshends Ledge #2, Cow and Calf #3, Taunton Rock #4, Branford Reef #5, and Brown's Reef #6.

East Breakwater #1

MORGAN POINT

FARM RIVER

Gong

Townshends Ledge #2

Cow and Calf #3

Bell

Taunton Rock #4

BRANFORD HARBOR

INDIAN NECK

Branford Reef #5

Beacon

THIMBLE ISLANDS

Bell

Brown's Reef #6

CHAPTER 23

Blackfish Holes
East Haven to Clinton

Editor's Note: Over the last eight seasons we've accumulated enough notes on places to fish to fill an encyclopedia—at least a small one. So, seeing how this is blackfishing season we decided to put some of our notes, past articles, discussions with tackle dealers, etc., to use. Please keep in mind these are not necessarily unknown spots, but neither are they barren. Keep them in mind the next time you're out. If your pet hole is dry that day, give one of these a try.

MAP #1: Spot #1 is the east breakwater of New Haven Harbor. Fish on the outside of the breakwater on the incoming and the inside of it on the outgoing tide. Another good spot here is the east end of the jetty. Spot #2 is Townshend Ledge. North of the gong is a piece of high bottom. Anchor your boat right on the high spot and start fishing. If that doesn't work try the east side of the gong. Spot #3 is the Cow and Calf, located to the SW of Branford Harbor entrance. Fish to the NW of the bell in 20 or so feet of water. Number 4 is Taunton Rock. Try some of the deeper edges here. This place is almost in the harbor. It could be in a lee on a certain wind. Number 5 is Branford Reef or the Beacon, as it's called by many. Fish about 50 yards to the NE of the Beacon. The first part of the incoming has been good here. Number 6 is Brown's Reef, located outside the Thimble Islands, to the SW. Try some of the deeper spots around the bell or just to the east of the nun buoy.

MAP #2: Spot #1 is Nettie's Reef. It's near the second black can outside the harbor. Fish along the east edge of this reef towards the channel. Try the incoming tide. Number 2 is Faulkner's Island. Fish both the north and south ends. Watch out on the north end. You don't want to fish in too far from the bell to the south because of submerged rocks. On the south side try in close to the island in 25' to 35' of water. Number 3 is Madison Reef. Incoming is also good here. Fish from 50 to 100 yards SE of the nun on the western end of the reef. Number 4 is Tuxis Island. Fish on the outside edges but watch the western corner as a rock sticks up there. Number 5 is south/southeast to the nun off Meigs Point Jetty. You can fish anywhere from in close to the buoy up to 100 yards out. Number 6 is the Clinton Breakwater off Kelsey Point. You can fish on either side but there's usually a lot of pots here (Map #2 on next page.)

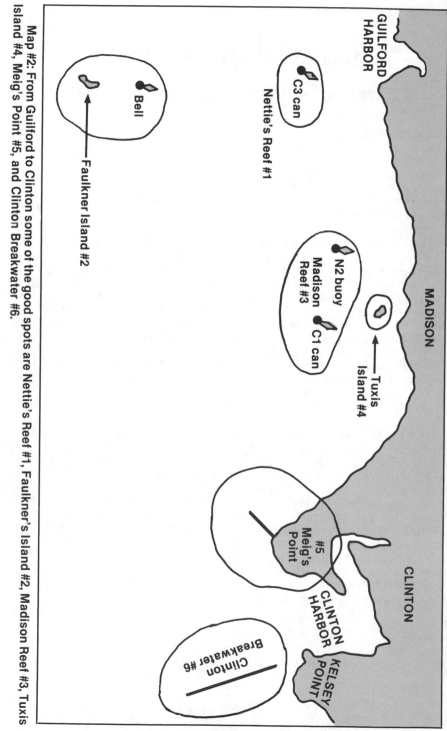

GUILFORD HARBOR

Nettie's Reef #1

C3 can

Bell

Faulkner Island #2

N2 buoy
Madison Reef #3
C1 can

Tuxis Island #4

MADISON

CLINTON

Meig's Point #5

CLINTON HARBOR

KELSEY POINT

Clinton Breakwater #6

Map #2: From Guilford to Clinton some of the good spots are Nettie's Reef #1, Faulkner's Island #2, Madison Reef #3, Tuxis Island #4, Meig's Point #5, and Clinton Breakwater #6.

CHAPTER 24

Day at Latimer's

Dave caught the first fish, and most of the ones in-between. His fishing partner for the day—alias the editor, alias the "big" striper fisherman who thought blackfish were always easy to catch—caught er, ah,...; let's just say somebody had to take the photos. Truth be known, Dave did the catchin'; Tim did the watchin'.

Dave in this case is Dave Motherway from Stonington. Besides being a quick man with the blackfish, Dave is also married to Mary Motherway—super do-it-all for *The Fisherman* office. Mary sliced through the editor's haze one morning at the office by saying Dave had a couple days off from work; would I be interested in going fishing? A phone call later confirmed the day, time, etc. Blackfishing at Latimer Reef Light looked like a good shot.

The morning of November 10 was a prize from the weatherman: light winds from the northeast and warm sun, with the promise of some finest kind of fishin'. Between now and Santa Claus we're not going to have too many more November 10 mornings. If one comes by, grab it and get out on the water.

First stop was to the west of the light in about thirty feet of water. Good tide running, but we picked the wrong bottom—no rocks. We reeled in the baits and the chum pot with a pint of cut-up, fresh-shucked sea clams in it. By 10:00 a.m., we'd tried a couple more spots to the east of the light without

Dave Motherway with one of several tautog he caught that day at Latimer Light.

a tap. The bottom was much better. The anchor chain clanked on the rocks below, but that was the only activity.

Next move brought us in close to the light on the southeast side. Dark water covered rocks below—a tautog condominium! Over went the chum pot and the baited rigs. Dave fished up in the bow, while the editor placed his bets astern. Twenty minutes went by without a touch. We were halfway through the pack of fig newtons when Dave gave a grunt. The light boat stick doubled over, then danced to the tune of a hooked tautog.

As the editor ate the fig newtons, tautog ate Dave's bait with increasing regularity. About the fifth fish, it became apparent Dave was doing something right, while what's-his-name in the stern was along for the ride. After unhooking his fifth fish, Dave mentioned he thought there was some type of hole up where he was fishing. The difference between our two lines was about ten to twelve feet.

A check of a chart showed a dropoff from seven to fifteen or so feet of water in the spot we occupied. Dave appeared to be fishing along the edge of the dropoff, while Big Bass Man was way out in no man's land. Dave politely inquired if Mr. Striper wouldn't care to come up toward the bow and possibly do a little something toward filling the fish box. Pride forgotten, the difference between our two lines narrowed to one foot. As soon as I lowered the rig, a fish gave two solid yanks. Nope, I didn't get him. The fish was just signalling to send down more crabs. At that point, I should have put away the rod and quit draining the bait supply.

If you moved the sinker around a little it would roll off the edge of the dropoff into deeper water. The fish were hanging along the edge. That morning three other boats fished the light: none took any fish.

It would be nice to report we just stayed put—no dice. We left on the editor's suggestion to try Middle Clump on the incoming tide. Considering what kind of a day it was, do you think my suggestion was a good one? After an hour-and-a-half without a touch, Dave was anxious to get back to the fish he'd been talked into leaving.

Not content to go right back to the fish, the editor further suggested trying outside of Latimer Reef in forty feet of water, by the red can. The tide was really rolling. Twelve ounces of lead held firm in the current. Another twenty minutes gone by. No fish. If empty time were tautog, I'd have had a boat full.

Finally, we got back in close to the light, to our previous spot. Down went the crabs—and the chum pot. Again a twenty minute wait, then the fish showed. And again the fish were along the dropoff. Lines on the port side caught fish. The starboard yielded a pot rope, but nothing else. Did I say lines? Yes, even you-know-who caught three fish: two throwbacks and one slammer of two pounds. Dave, meanwhile, caught four more nice ones.

The fish weren't really taking the bait aggressively. The hits were more like your sinker had moved—only it was a fish. A change of bait to sea clams produced some very nice cunners, but no blacks. The crabs were what they wanted. You had to be on your toes to detect too soft hits. Dave's rod arched over once again. The editor set the hooks into a sizeable portion of the reef that he was unable to boat. Up on the abandoned light, a seagull squawked in amusement.

Try, try again. Another fifteen minutes and two fish turned over, but lost. What was wrong? Remember the reef; can't hook a fish with the point bent in. A pair of pliers was what I needed. So did Dave—he had to get the hook out of another fish.

At about the time the sun got ready to exit, Dave said he'd really enjoyed the day. The editor meanwhile was busy trying to move Latimer Reef again. Originally, we'd planned to leave at 4 p.m. because Dave had to pick up some lumber. It wouldn't make any sense to leave until all the crabs were used up, right? That was the mark of a good fisherman: good, plausible excuses to get out of work, thought up in minimal time. We stayed put.

About the time a sailboat crossed broadside to the retreating sun, Dave mentioned Rock Island as a future spot to try for blacks. He also passed along the word he'd taken some nice flats between the island and the second red can to the south. When flats were tough to come by, that stretch of bottom was a good bet.

The last of the crabs came and went. Time to leave for a few brews and supper. Back at the house, Dave iced the fish until the morning, when he'd be in much better shape to do a good job of filleting and skinning. Don't try to scale blackfish. Get a pair of pliers and pull the skin off the meat. If you ice the fish overnight it's a good idea to place them in a cooler with a drain. Tilt the cooler so the melted ice water drains out; otherwise the water will make a soggy mess of your catch.

Supper consisted of buttered noodles, meat sauce, corn, Italian bread and c-o-l-d beer. Dave couldn't get over what a prime trip it had been. The editor, meanwhile, was rather silent. He just sat there content to munch on his sizeable portion of crow.

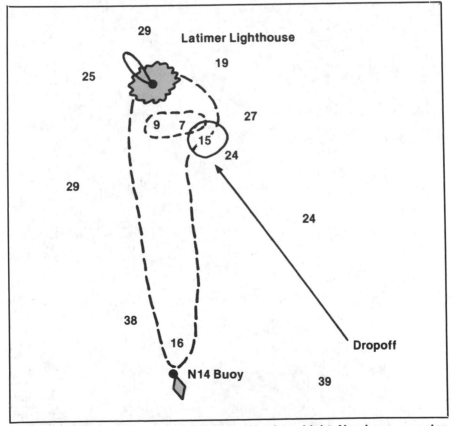

Here's an approximation of the reef off Latimer Light. Numbers are water depths and dotted lines are the approximate bottom contours. Circle is the dropoff where fish were holding. You had to be right on the edge.

After a long night of bassfishing, a regular loads a trophy into the back of his truck.

CHAPTER 25

Three-Way Eeling

Looking for some bass this fall? In the next month or so many fish over 30 lbs. will fall. A goodly number of them will go to boats using live bait during the day or eels at night.

On the latter, if you have an eye on some spots in 20' to 50' of water, you might try three-waying. It's nothing new. Anglers fishing the series of rips off New London, CT called The Race, have used the method for years. The tons of big fish caught there are a testimonial to its effectiveness.

The three-way rig gets its name from the use of a three-way swivel as the centerpiece. The rig is tied up around it. When it's finished, it looks to some like a fluke rig only it's intended for bass in deeper water on a running tide.

The rig is simple to construct. Start with a 1/0 size three-way swivel. On one eye tie a 4' to 5' piece of 60-80 lb. test mono. On the end of this tie a 9/0 Claw style hook. On one other eye of the swivel tie a 24" to 30" piece of mono. Here there are two schools of thought. Some use line lighter than that being used on the reel. The idea is the light line will break before the main line when you get hung up. This way you lose only part of a rig. Others just rig the sinker on 60 or 80 lb. They feel the heavier line lets them break away sinkers they might otherwise lose. If the sinker doesn't come away, they just break off and tie on another rig. If you are three-waying on some broken bottom, plan on losing rigs. It's part of the game.

Some readers might question the length from swivel to sinker. Thirty inches sounds à bit long. The answer to that was given by a fellow who lives

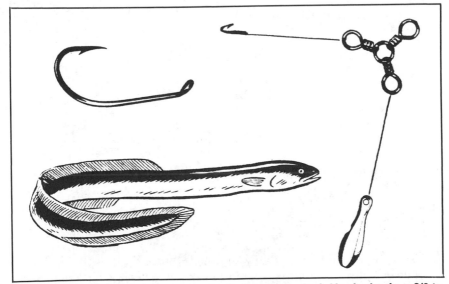

Three-way rig is made up around a three-way swivel. Hook size is a 6/0 to 7/0 claw style; sinker weight can be anywhere from 2 to 20 ounces. Length of leader from swivel eye to hook is usually 4 to 5 feet while from other eye of swivel to sinker is 24 to 30 inches.

in Sag Harbor, Long Island and regularly fishes Plum Gut, a tide rip close to The Race. He told employees of our sister publication, The Long Island Fisherman, that the long sinker lead helps keep the eel up off the bottom a bit. As such, it's more in the line of sight of a bass holding out of the current behind a rock. Remember, a bass' eyes are geared more toward looking up than looking down. The fish is likely to see somthing going over her head close by. Also, with the eel riding a bit higher there's less chance the hook will get caught in low-lying rocks.

Generally heavier tackle is used for three-waying. In The Race, sinkers up to 20 oz. are necessary to stay down on strong tides. In other areas, 2 to 4 oz. might be fine, say, during the end of a tide. A good starter outfit would be a high speed 3/0 or 4/0 reel, rod somewhere from 30 to 50 lb. class trolling blank and 40 to 50 lb. mono. In time you might want to go lighter. This past August, I had some good sport with 30 lb. fish on a Shimano graphite musky rod rated for 20 to 40 lb. line and lure or sinker weights of 4-8 oz. You also in time might consider dacron line, especially if you are in deeper water. Fifty pound dacron is much more popular than mono in The Race where bass are consistently hooked in water deeper than 50 feet.

Best results with three-waying are usually made when the eel is down close to the bottom. Some anglers favor the sinker banging the bottom. Others drop the rig down then crank in a few turns. Another case has fish that hold at mid-depths. One such place where this happens is the North Rip of Block Island. Here you might drop the rig down, put the reel in gear, then just drift along without letting out more line in an effort to stay near the bottom.

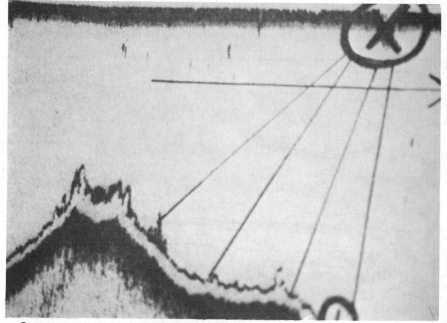

Once you clear the top of the reef you can fish down the back of it by taking the reel out of gear and letting out line as the bottom drops away. The X with the circle represents a drifting boat, the arrow the direction of the tide and the small line inside the circle was a bass. I say was because she was caught thanks to a three-way rig.

One accepted method of hooking an eel is through both lips, starting underneath, then bringing the point out the top of the head. You'll need a rag to purchase a hold on the slippery bait. Some regulars wrap the eel in a rag, then whack it across the gunwale a couple times. This slows the eel down for hooking and also prevents him tangling up in the line. It doesn't in any way reduce its effectiveness.

A lot of three-way fishing is done in rips. These could be situated off a point of land on the ocean side of an island; perhaps there's a high spot in the bottom a little way offshore or perhaps it's a rip at the mouth of a river. One usually runs uptide, drops the rig down to bottom, then allows the tide to push your boat back into the rip. In some cases fish hold uptide, while in other cases they will be behind. On a lot of nights you might find a pocket of fish holding in one small section. This brings up a couple points. Number one, you might have to thoroughly fish the whole rip before deciding fish are not present. Just drifting over a couple spots in 500' of rip is not advisable unless you know for sure fish only hold in a few set spots. There's not as many fish as 5 to 10 years ago.

Once located, you have to make another pass over the same small spot. That's easier said than done in the dark. If you found fish on the deeper edges of the rip, you can locate them by height of the rip itself. If fish were in the center, height again can help. Besides height you might get back to your first spot by putting a buoy in line with a shore light, then running uptide from that. If you are close enough to a can you might judge a range on position and distance from the navigational aid.

While shore ranges can help greatly, you won't really know for sure unless you have a chart machine. By drifting with it running you have a permanent record of the spot of your first found fish. If your next drift doesn't produce about the same bottom contour, keep looking.

Wind also plays a part, especially if you are out in a small, lightweight boat. If a breeze is quartering the tide, this might have to be taken into account in where to start another drift. As the tide eases, wind might become more of a factor in your movement. You might have to constantly rearrange your drift pattern to take that into consideration. The opposite is true as a tide gathers strength, taking control of your craft from the wind.

If fish are holding behind a rip line, you might have to let out more line as the water gets deeper. You feel right away if the sinker has been in contact with bottom. Having a chart machine running will also let you know such is happening. Keep dropping back the rig. This will "walk" the eel down the hill perhaps to a 50 lb. fish holding in a pocket out of the main flow of the tide. The ability to immediately follow the bottom contour is one of the main attributes of three-waying.

Last point on rip fishing is tide. You might be in the right church but services might not start until the last couple of hours. Big, lazy bass have a habit of hitting on the slacker stages of tide. It's easier for them to feed. If you fished a known spot unproductively during the middle of the tide, it might be wise to make a couple passes later on.

In travels around New England this summer, I saw, or was told about, places where three-waying sounds like it might work. The mouth of the Merrimac River in Newburyport or off Race Point on Cape Cod sound like good possibilities. Keep in mind three-waying has been used successfully in the deeper sections off Watch Hill, Rhode Island; in Block Island's North Rip; Quick's Hole just behind the can past North Rock and Great Point Rip on Nantucket. Any place where bass are in deep water or swift tides is a possible target for live eels on a three-way rig.

CHAPTER 26

Cornfield Point Surf Fishing

"A fifty from shore isn't an impossibility...I once had a fish on here for 35 minutes...That same night I got some teen blues and a 16 pound bass...The blues took 15 minutes to land."

Fellow in a wet suit with an orange windbreaker over top of it said that to me a couple weeks ago. We stood atop slimy rocks alongside a swirling rip. As you stand on the tip of the point all the water in a shallow bay washes past your feet on an ebb tide. If you're lucky, you'll have someone like Pat Abate in his wet suit beside you, showing you how to fish Cornfield Point.

Cornfield Point consistently produces big bass and blues, though naturally some years are better than others. Check page 34 of the October 11, 1973 issue of The Long Island Fisherman. Skip Fleet's column gave the

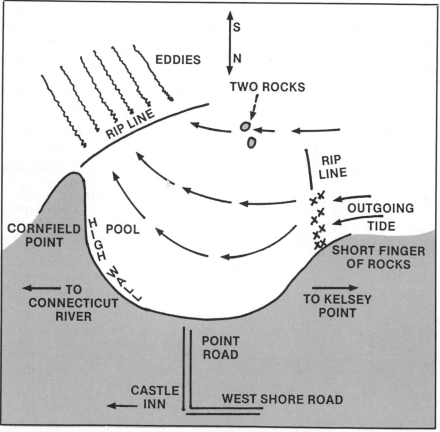

Layout of Cornfield Point as it would be on an outgoing tide.

rundown on a fellow member of The Connecticut River Striped Bass Club taking fish up to 51 pounds from a boat right in close in this area. During 1973 Pat Abate lost his fight with that first paragraph bass. Thirty-five minutes on heavy spinning tackle cranked by a seasoned fisherman means a leg-shaker of a striper. Fish that size require hundreds of hours work for a shorefisherman to meet up with. Unfortunately, it wasn't in the cards that night; too bad, for Pat's an accomplished plug man who deserved better.

Look on page 17 of the October 16, 1975 issue of The Connecticut Rhode Island Fisherman and you see the same sort of thing occurring at Cornfield. One member of Skip's Club got some 15-16 pound blues while another guy got a 25 pound bass; both from shore. Cornfield isn't the promised land; matter of fact, this year wasn't as productive as previous seasons. But anybody seriously interested in Connecticut surf fishing shouldn't leave this place uninvestigated too long during a season.

Surf fishing in Connecticut is a skill practiced by guys receiving little notice about their catches. I know of several nice hauls made from the shore so far this season. If numbers and locations were known, I'm sure some of the traveling buggy fishermen elbowing for room along the hard side of Charlestown Breachway would turn as green as one color of their Gibbs mackerel swimmers.

Anyway, Cornfield doesn't seem to be the type place always having a fish or two around. Cornfield either has a body of fish or is barren. This generalization holds true year in and year out, not on one given night.

To reach this point get off 95 at the Old Saybrook Exit. Take route One to the Old Boston Post Rd. You can only turn one way (Chevron gas on the corner). Take the Post Rd. about ½ block to Conn. Rte. 154. Again, you can only turn one way. Follow 154 over the Back River, past the town beach to Ridge Rd. Conn. 154 makes a sharp turn to the left just before the intersection. Make a right on Ridge Rd. Go two stop signs to Town Beach Rd. Make a right. Go one block to the water, make a left. Go a short distance on West Shore Rd. to Point Rd. Make a left, drive 300 feet to park behind the Castle Inn (looks just like a castle).

Once arrived, don't let the world know how much beer you had to drink awaiting the tide. Nothing closes accesses faster than loud noise, garbage on the ground or some jamoke watering the roses right under a streetlight at three in the morning. People owning property close to productive spots take only so much of this behavior, then call the cops.

After you quietly exit your car walk south about 500 feet to the water. Climb down to the water's edge at the end of the street. Don't walk along the high wall running off to your left. It's private property.

To your right is a short finger of rocks running out a short distance to the south. Directly in front of you is a pool. To your left is rocky Cornfield Point. On an outgoing tide water in the shallow, U-shaped bay between Kelsey and Cornfield Points flows northwest to southeast. The tide flows past Chalker Beach, then past Plum Bank Beach, then out past Cornfield toward Long Sand Shoal.

As the water moves over that first, short finger of rocks, a small tide rip forms. The water then flows into the pool and out over submerged rocks lying northeast to southwest, directly across the path of the outgoing tide. The tide is forced up over these rocks, resulting in a fishy-looking rip.

Both sides of Cornfield Point have 8 to 17 foot depths a short distance from shore. The combination of water depth, tide rip and outflow of bait attracts fish to the area. In addition there's numerous shoals and reefs to the south and southeast of the point to hold fish. On more than one tide fish from Cornfield Point Shoal (700 yards south of the point) move right up the rip to the tip of Cornfield Point.

Most of your bass hit on the downtide side of the second, more pronounced rip. Best method for bass is a quartering cast across the current toward the southwest. Let the tide carry a swimmer or eel back into the calmer eddies behind the rip line. Once you think your lure is far enough back, start a slow retrieve. You standardize the length of each drift by slowly counting as the current carries your plug or eel away from you.

Try counting in multiples of ten. Make your first couple drifts at ten count, next couple leave out to twenty and so on. Don't be afraid to try high or low tide slack water. Cast all around the point at such times not just the western side.

If you float a surface swimming plug way back into the quiet water on a quiet night, try popping the plug across the top. Three nights previous to my last trip to Cornfield I put in a couple hours one night at Matunuck. I fished the rocks to the east of Deep Hole. Twenty minutes casting in one spot by some pilings produced nothing. Next couple casts I popped as well as

This photo was taken at Cornfield on a Saturday morning during the last part of the outgoing tide.

swam the plug slowly across the top. Third cast I hooked and dropped a fish about ten pounds in the pancake water. Five casts later I had another hit, but missed him. Doubt if there'd been any action, save for popping a swimmer.

You also get stubborn fish to hit by repeated casting of a noisy popper to a spot you know there's fish milling around. If a bass comes up but won't hit, keep throwing the popper in the same spot about 20 to 30 consecutive casts. If you've got the patience, sometimes you'll get a very mad fish.

On the average you get more fish at Cornfield on the outgoing, though Skip Fleet told me he pulled out one night on low slack, leaving two guys from Hartford Surf there to do a little house-cleaning. The next morning Skip got a call about incoming tides and 9 blues plus 3 more bass he walked away from.

Waders are better than hip boots for fishing Cornfield. You can wade out far enough so your line doesn't bend around rocks as the plug or eel swings downtide with the current. With chest highs you get out beyond those troublesome, line-fraying rocks.

Bluefishermen score casting into the pool or toward the two rocks sticking up to the east of the tip of the point or right in the second rip. Poppers are the popular choice though some guys do well on the blues with big swimmers after dark. Bunker chunks fished in the pool get blues also.

If you're at the point when a school of big bunkers come through, try to snag one. For consistency nothing beats a snagged bunker wiggling amongst his untouched brothers. Big bass and blues home right in on the cripple.

Best shore snagging rig I've seen was a Kastmaster or Hopkins with a treble on the rear and another treble clipped to snap at the head of the lure. The extra treble prevents you from smacking a bunker with the blunt end of the metal.

Regular boat snagging rigs don't work too well from shore because the extra hooks are always snagging in the rocky bottom. Also, blues can get their teeh around the leader. Recently a friend of mine got into bass and blues into bunker packed into Deep Hole on the 10th of October. He hooked four nice fish before dark by snagging bunker with two stainless steel trebles rigged on 80 pound test Steelon ahead on a four ounce sinker.

First fish, a nice bass, grabbed the bunker but was lost because the sinker dangling from the rig fouled in the bottom when the fish dove. The next fish was a 17 pound blue. The next blue bit the bunker right in half and the last blue right through the Steelon.

It's tough for a blue to come all the way up over a big bunker plus a length of metal lure. The lure acts as insurance against the first blue but there's nothing to prevent a second piranha from taking a shine at that edible looking morsel protruding from his brother's mouth.

One evening at Cornfield I snagged somebody else's recently lost bait rig. The bunker chunk hadn't started to decompose. I chucked it over my shoulder to be picked up later. Two hours later you couldn't find the chunk for all the green crabs feasting on it. Such abundance of crabs is the reason numberous blackfish are caught in the pool between the rips.

At times you'll find an abundance of fishermen at Cornfield, especially when outgoing coincides with dust or with daybreak on the weekends. At other times you show up under the streetlight at 2 A.M., hopcfully rcady for uncrowded fishing.

If you see a guy with a black wet suit and one of those three-block long spinning rigs so favored at Montauk, say, "Hey, Pat." If the guy answers, "Yeah whatcha want," tell him Tim said hello.

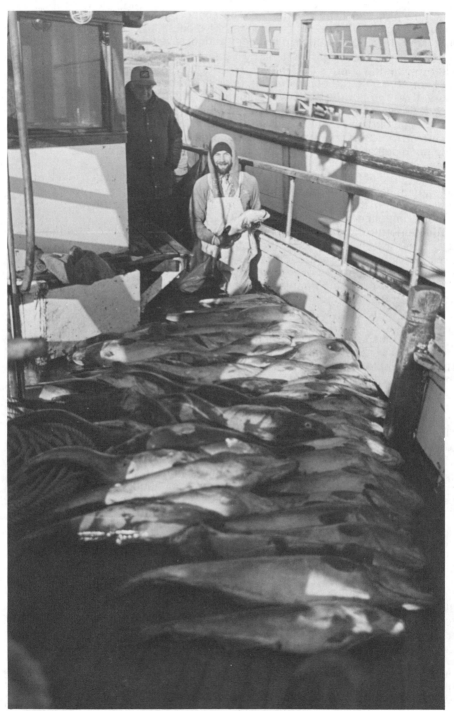

Rich DeRise with a fine catch of cod made off Block Island just prior to Christmas.

CHAPTER 27

Christmas Cod

Years ago around Christmas, I bumped into George and his wife at the Mystic Pharmacy. George wanted to know how the codfishing had been. Rather than tell him, I said I'd leave a Polaroid shot of the last trip tacked to the inside of our office window; he could see for himself. Two days later, George was out off Block Island.

Fishing on the Block Island grounds during the three weeks prior to Christmas of 1978 was good. It built to a peak just before the holiday. On December 23 and 24, fishing was super. On the twenty-third, my total was thirty-two cod and one pollack, from eight to twenty-four pounds.

Unfortunately, the bubble broke. On Christmas Day, 1978, a strong storm descended on our region. The following day we returned to the same site of the slaughter of two days before. The fish were gone.

Christmas cod of 1979 were not nearly as good. There were some decent catches, but the fish were more scattered around. Strong NW winds also hampered operations on several trips. Better catches were made by the headboats on days when the wind didn't blow. It was too bad, for they were carrying well. The word of the year before's numbers made the rounds. Expectant anglers were out in force looking for a repeat.

On December 27, 1979, both Point Judith boats were out to the SE of the island. A strong NW wind was getting worse. With the wind and the tide together, all lines went back toward the stern. Our boat had gone over a hump, run up-wind, then came back on the anchor line. When the boat settled in, the stern was right atop the hump. Anyone who dropped a rig straight down had a much better chance at a cod or two. Those who cast away from

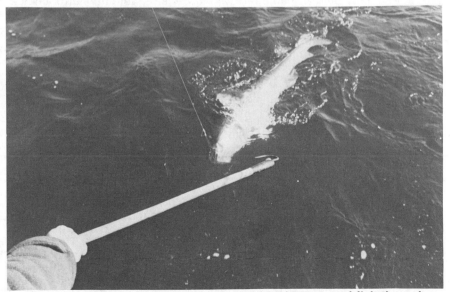

This particular year one private boat had a nice mess of fish three days before Christmas at SW Ledge.

the stern battled choggies. However, after one hour we had to move, leaving a fair pick of small fish.

Stong NW winds spoiled more than just one Christmas cod trip. On several days, the two boats made their way out to the south or southeast of the island in the morning, but got only an hour or so there. They eventually sought shelter in the lee of Block Island. There were some fish around, but the blasted wind put the screws to it.

On some days there were cod in fair to good numbers in close to the island. One Saturday about mid-month there was a school of fish moving off SE Light. We had them on the Julie-C for awhile, but they moved on. The same day another fellow aboard a Montauk boat in the same area took some nice fish, including a forty pounder that grabbed a hooked whiting on the way up. On December 22, a private boat had a fair mess of cod at Southwest Ledge. On December 24 another private boat took twenty-eight cod to forty pounds off Clay Head. Fish were there, but not in the consistent, concentrated numbers of the year before. In between trips mentioned here, there were others where fishing was poor.

After Christmas, the cold weather really became a factor. The last entry in my log for a Christmas cod story was on January 4, 1980. One charter boat on a busman's holiday jigged up some medium fish at Nebraska Shoal.

In 1979, the dogfish of November were mostly gone by the first part of December. On occasion, they made the usual pests of themselves like on December 23, The trip before the Super Squirrel made a pretty good day on Coxes with some nice pollack and cod. The next day, both the Squirrel and Julie-C returned to the same numbers. The bottom was full of dogfish. Each time one or the other skipper located a pick of small fish, the doggies moved in. I'd like to see the gillnetters zero in exclusively on the dogs. Both parties deserve each other.

In 1978, jigging with a red tube and eight ounce Norway style jig far out-produced clams. On the head boats, at least, clams were the better choice in 1979. One trip at mid-December in close off SE Light, one fellow got around the choggies by baiting with mackerel. He got them from a lone jigger who'd taken a solitary twenty pound cod plus twenty-five big mackerel. At times during the morning, the mackerel wouldn't let the jig hit bottom. Anyway, the enterprising baitfisherman cut chunks out of one of the mackerel and took three cod from eight to twelve pounds in as many drops. The day before, in about the same location, three of eight fares near the stern used jigs. One fellow (guess who?) had a nine ounce jig; the other two had twelve ouncers. Between the two of them they caught five cod. The dumbo with the lighter jig got zip. We were only in about sixty feet of water, but the heavier jigs made the difference. While the jigs were producing, fish were also coming up with bait. The school only stayed around thirty minutes.

On December 28, three of us went out on the Super Squirrel. We had a pretty good shot of small fish to the east of the island on a morning with moderate wind. Jigging yielded nothing until late in the day when we moved to a piece of bottom nicknamed the Apple Tree. The same dumbo as before refused to try the jig anymore as it produced nothing. Another Tim aboard was stubborn though. He gave the "iron clam" one more try. He flipped the jig away from the port side and let it settle. Two lifts and he had a twenty-five pounder stuck in one eyeball. Another fare noticed his success. Instead of fishing a twelve ounce Norway jig near the bottom, this man slowly squidded a six ounce Ava with tube up ahead. About fifteen slow turns were on the reel when his rod went over on a double of ten pound pollack. That was it, though, for jigs.

What will the future bring? Your guess is as good as mine. Don't be discouraged if you were on one of the poor trips last Christmas. Some people out then told me pretty vocally they thought reports of 1978 the figment of my pet bull. It wasn't.

It may be cold that time of year but some seasons it is well worth the effort.

If you are serious about live bait fishing, one of the best ways to get bunker is with a 100 foot section of gillnet.

CHAPTER 28

Gillnetting Bunker

Editor's Note: The use of gillnets may be illegal in some states or require a bait license in others. Check local regulations to be sure.

This time of year getting bunker can sometimes be a problem if you have only a snagging rig. The schools are often sparse. You might have to work for literally hours trying to get even a half dozen baits.

Lately some of the harder working fishermen have been getting around this by use of gillnets, usually purchased from a commercial supply house in one hundred foot lengths. One angler I know sets his net two hours each morning before first light. By the time sunrise comes, he usually has plenty of bait to start fishing.

One enterprising bassman - and a reader of The Fisherman - recently agreed to show how he uses a gillnet and to supply some bits of info about the net itself.

He got the net over at Wilcox Marine in Stonington. The section is one hundred feet long, nine feet high from the cork line to lead line and has three inch mesh. The net is made out of monofilament and the filaments of the net look to be equal to about twenty pound test line.

The top part of his net is a cork line. That's a series of corks strung on a one hundred foot length of rope. The net is fastened to this rope and hangs down from it in the water. The bottom part of the net is a lead line. This is a one hundred foot length of rope with lead weights on it. The net is also fastened to this rope. The lead causes the bottom section to sink - and stay down. The corks, however, will not be pulled under. This is how the net stays open, top to bottom; corks to keep it afloat and lead weights to make the net hang straight down.

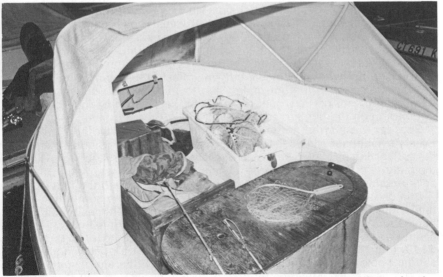

When not in use the net is stored in a plastic fish box placed up under the forward canvas so it is out of the sun.

This particular net is stored in one of the heavy plastic fish boxes seen mainly in commercial packing houses. Since it is important to keep a mono gillnet out of the sun, the net and box are stored up under the spray hood of a 19' Aquasport. The sun will cause the mono to become brittle; thus it will break much easier.

On the far end of the net (the end which goes out first when it is set), my friend ties two, sixteen ounce sinkers to the lead line. These weights hold that end of the net in place. On the other end is a fifteen foot section of cord tied to the last portion of the cork line. Once the net has been set, the cord is tied to one handrail of the console.

Before setting a net in the dark it's a good idea to make a good dry run in the daylight. Don't be surprised if this takes a little work before you get the hang of it.

The first step in this whole operation is to locate some bunkers - in the dark. You can do this either by running over an area at low speed with your chart recorder, or listen for flips on a still night. Next step is to check which way the wind or tide will push the net and boat once you make a set. If there is no wind or little tide, you will probably have to put the engine in gear. As the boat moves slowly along, let out the net, watching to make sure it doesn't catch on anything as it slips over the gunwale. It is best to have a fairly clear working area.

Once my friend had set his net, and tied the leader to the console rail, you could hold the leader in your hand and feel bunker bumping into the mesh. At times when several bunker hit one section at once, the cork line would take a V-shape at that point.

He never left the net in the water more than ten minutes per set. Any longer and he figured the baits would suffocate. When a bunker gets gilled in such a net, he can't breathe by opening and closing his gills. If he's left in that position for too long he'll die.

The net was retrieved by first pulling the cork line up out of the water. Then he'd reach down and grab the lead line, bringing the two lines together. Once he had them both in his hands, he'd pull in a section of net and coil it neatly in the plastic fish box. He'd repeat this hauling procedure until all the net was in. It's important to retrieve the net this way because if it is stored evenly, it will go back out without any major tangles.

When my friend came to a bunker, he'd push it through the mesh, then slip it into his bait tank that had a pump circulating water through it. He used to use a net with 3¾" mesh, but was missing too many smaller baits. With that size mesh, he got mainly ten to thirteen inch bunker.With the three inch mesh, he now gets more of the seven to nine inch baits that swam through the larger mesh.

One day we started netting at 5:30 a.m.; by 7 a.m., we had twenty to twenty five baits in the tank. During the morning, medium blues did a job on the bait, giving us back plenty of heads. My friend kept at it, though. Right in the middle of the blues, up came a twenty-two pound bass. Without all the backup bunker, I doubt if he could have "waded" through the bluefish.

One aspect of baitfishing that has always soured me somewhat is the time it SOMETIMES took to snag bait. There were more times than I like to think about when we got to the grounds long after the prime time of the first couple hours of daylight had passed. The only thing doing (or so it seemed) was a four pound blue with an uncanny skill to eat a bunker rigged with stinger hook and not end up in the fish box. With the aid of a gillnet, an angler has a much, much better shot at having enough bait to start fishing at first light.

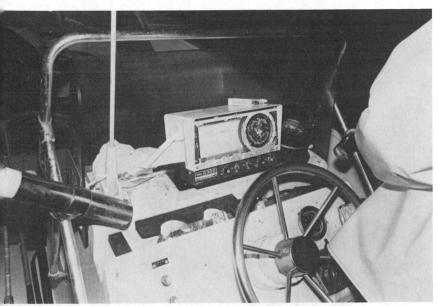

You can locate schools of bunker at night, even when they are not flipping on top, by using your chart recorder. They'll show up as heavy black lines if there's enough of them. Even when bunker are scattered, a gillnet is the most efficient way to get them.

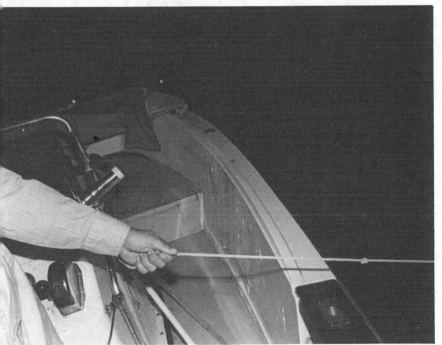

If you hold the leader to the net you can feel bunker bumping into the mesh.

Author with bass of 29 and 47 pounds taken casting an Atom 40 on the south end of Menunketesuck Island.

CHAPTER 29

Islands off Westbrook

The major credit for this information goes to my friend, Phil Wetmore, a lifelong resident of Westbrook. Phil has fished this area since he was a kid. This story is the result of conversations with him and a couple of recent trips in a Brockway skiff the week of August 17, plus other outings over the last four years.

To get a better idea of the nooks and crannies mentioned here, get hold of Chart 12374 covering Duck Island to Madison Reef. The chart marked up for this story was that one. The two islands are Menunketesuck (pronounced Mae-nun-kay-tea-sick) and Duck Islands; respectively, they lie to the southeast and south of the mouth of the Patchogue and Menunketesuck Rivers in the Town of Westbrook.

Let's take a look at Menunketesuck first. By the way, this area is pretty much restricted to boat casting because of the distance of the island from shore. In the case of Duck Island, it is impossible to get there without a boat. Menunketesuck is a long sliver of land extending from the northwest to southeast. A broad cut separates the island from the mainland. At the top of the tide, there's five to six feet of water in this cut.

Along the tip of the island (marked #1 on the story chart) are sections of eel grass. In this spot, try casting poppers or swimmers right on the top of the flood tide. Fish often go up into the grass looking for chow. This is mostly schoolie country, but every once in a while a cow gets into the act. Phil had one of his customers take a forty-nine pounder trolling a live eel on mono along the western tip of the eel grass. Smaller lures like the five-and-a-half inch Rebel or RedFin or one ounce popping plugs will work here.

Next area is a short rock jetty on the eastern side of the island out toward the end (this is marked #2). Lay off from the jetty and cast plugs or eels into this stretch. If the water is calm, try a surface swimmer like the Danny Atom Jr., or 40. If there's some chop, try the biggest Cordell RedFin or some other subsurface swimmer. Live eels are good, but bluefish prowl here, so be prepared to get back a lot of "cigar butts." This spot is good on the flood tide about two hours near high, with a slight wind from the northeast. Blues will definitely come your way, but so will bass over twenty-five pounds.

Number three is called Three Rocks by Phil. As you move out away from the southern tip of the island, you should notice three rocks arranged in a somewhat triangular fashion in four to five feet of water at the top of the incoming tide. The southern-most rock in this triangle is the last rock out you see sticking up at high tide. Right between those three rocks is a good place to cast a surface swimmer like the Atom 40 or big Danny. Back in October, 1974, I was lucky enough to yank a 47 lb. 12 oz. bass and other fish from those rocks on an Atom. Phil says he's always done better in this spot on the incoming tide.

I know this is primarily an article on where to cast plugs, but yet couldn't help throwing in #4. This is a dropoff from nine to sixteen to twenty-plus feet of water. On the moving tide, this is a good bet for wire line and bucktails. The catch - on a yearly basis - will be mostly blues, but also some twenty to thirty pound bass. If you are in the area on a full moon, you might try wiring some big plugs at night.

Before we go on, here's a tip: if you put say, a surface swimmer on target, but the fish merely comes up, swirls under the lure but won't "make a purchase," try casting dead center to the spot another dozen or so casts. If the fish won't get mad enough to come after the surface swimmer, try a subsurface plug from a different direction. That means positioning your boat differently in relation to whatever rock the fish is holding by. Say the lure was orginally hit coming away from the eastern side of the island in a west-to-east direction. For uncooperative bass, try a different lure coming up on him from, say, a northwest to southeast movement. Be as quiet as you can when you move the boat, keeping chances of spooking him to a minimum.

Some casters like to drift while others quietly get in as close as they can, then throw the anchor. The former anglers usually work a place over with one or two casts, then drift on. The latter school of thought fishes a place for perhaps fifteen minutes to a half an hour, then seeks greener pastures. It's been my experience the latter technique is best when fish are holding on the end of an island, right in the face of a tide rip. Here is the best chance for anchoring and casting since the fish often move up and down the rip looking for chow.

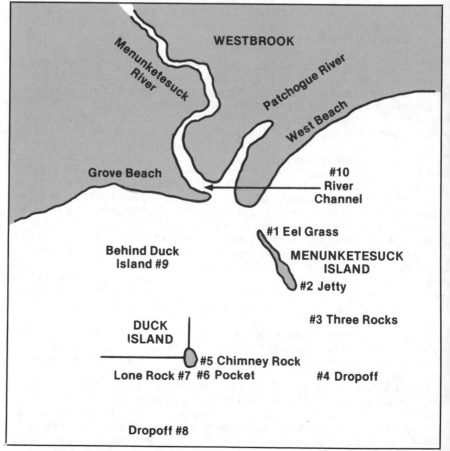

Here's ten different locations to fish for bass and blues around Westbrook. See story for details.

From here we go over to Duck Island. Two man-made breakwaters extend out from the northern and eastern tips of the island, creating a nice harbor between them. During the summer and fall months, a lot of pleasure boaters pull in here for a break.

As you look over the island from this harbor, one can't help but notice a chimney sticking up from about dead center on the island. This is the remains of who-knows-what. It does conveniently mark a deep hole on the eastern side of the island. As you face the chimney (from out in a boat) from the east, you will notice a big rock at the high water mark. Right out in front of this rock is a ten foot hole. Lay off this patch of water and cast a plug or eel in here. If there's anybody home you should know about it. Flood tide, up near the top of the tide, is a good bet.

Next locale is right out near the tip of the island. Look #6 on the chart accompanying the story. Here is a good spot to anchor up. As you approach the southern tip of the island on an incoming flood tide, you should see a pocket formed by three big rocks spaced at irregular intervals. You want to set your boat so you can lob plugs in that pocket and right around the stones. At a halfway point in the tide, the furthest rock out is under water with a big boil marking its presence. Easy does it the first time. Don't go in here at night unless you know what's where. Remember inflation and the cost of a new lower unit.

One night out with Phil, I had a good bluefish speedily come up to a Danny, then just as speedily cut me off behind one of the rocks we just talked about. Needless to say, I wasn't too pleased with myself. A phone call the next day, to one of the regulars in this area told of some hummer blues to fifteen pounds then prowling the Duck Island rip. Fifteen pounds or less, the choppers were eating everything from plugs to bucktails.

When you are in a position in the pocket, look a little behind the rip line in close to shore. You should see one lone rock sticking up out of the water; this rock is behind or to the west of the pocket. On the incoming tide, this is a good spot to pick up a bass or two. One of the fellows who keeps his boat at Phil's place has always caught bass near this rock with popping plugs. A swimmer wouldn't hurt the effort either.

Number eight again slips back into the realm of the troller. You see the drop off on the chart from nine to sixteen, then down to twenty feet? That's a good spot to snap bucktails and pork rind for bass; blues also. Incoming tide would be a good time to try.

Our next stop is behind Duck Island. At night bunkers, with blues right on their tails, move in here. On a still night you can hear fish working over the bait. I really couldn't pinpoint any single section of water, since the bait will go almost any place to escape the chopping blues. If you find a school of bunker on top in a tightly packed circle, throw a plug like the Goo Goo Eyes Big Daddy in there. This lure will go under the bunker right in line of sight of blues attacking the school from below.

At times the blues push the bunker right up into the mouth of the two rivers. On some still nights, people who have houses near the left channel (#10) hear splashes as blues (and bass?) have a late night meal. Any time fish are feeding like that it is an opportunity to catch them with plugs. On a still, quiet night you might get them with a big surface swimmer. I imagine boat traffic must be at a minimum for the fish to come in here.

That's it. I'm out of info. At that point in my talks with Phil, he got up and left to go watch the Red Sox; yours truly left to go back to Mystic to put this on paper. If you leave to go fishing, get some plugs and go try off Westbrook.

View of state ramp in Westport, Conn. Photo by Dick Alley

CHAPTER 30

Saltwater Launch Ramps

Branford—Branford River: On Branford River approximately 2 miles south of Branford Center. Turn south off Rte. 1 onto Rte. 142. Steep ramp.

Bridgeport—Seaside Park: Seaside Park on west side of Bridgeport Harbor, approximately 1½ miles south of I-95. Poor launch conditions.

Groton—Bayberry Lane: On Bakers Cover, 2½ miles southeast of Groton and one mile east of Coast Guard Station.

Groton—Thames River (Kenneth E. Streeter): Travel I-95 northbound to Bridge Street Exit. Bear right at end of exit. Follow Bridge Street until it ends. Turn right onto Fairview Avenue. Launch is under I-95 on south side of Fairview Avenue. Or, I-95 southbound to Kings Highway Exit. Take Kings Highway to Bridge Street; then, same as above.

Guilford—East River: Travel south from U.S. 1 on Neck Road approximately 1½ miles. Located on east bank of East, 3 miles southwest of Madison. Paved ramp, good launch conditions.

New Haven—Lighthouse Point: In Lighthouse Point Park, approximately 3 miles south of I-95. Launching should present no problems except in strong wind directly out of west.

Madison—Hammonasset Beach (Meigs Point): 1 mile south of Exit 62 from Rt. I-95. Follow signs to Hammonasset Beach State Park. Launching over sandy beach.

Milford—Housatonic River: Under the I-95 Bridge in Devon. Turn north from Rte. 1 onto Naugatuck Avenue. Good launch conditions.

The ramp at Niantic is a good jumping off spot for anglers who wish to fish at Plum Gut, Bartletts or The Race.

This is the state ramp at Barn Island in the town of Stonington, Conn.

New London—Thames River: Follow Main Street to Crystal Avenue. Launch is on "Old Bridge Approach" directly under I-95 on the west side of the river. Follow signs to "State Pier."

Old Lyme—Four Mile River: On west side of Four Mile River opposite Rocky Neck State Park and approximately 1½ miles south of Rte. 156. Shallow launch conditions at low tide, clearance problem at high tide.

Old Lyme—Great Island: At south end of Smith Neck Road approximately one mile south of Rte. 156 and 2½ miles south of U.S. 1 and the Baldwin Bridge.

Old Saybrook—Connecticut River (Baldwin Bridge): Under Baldwin Bridge (I-95). Cement ramp with pads.

Stonington—Barn Island: Turn southeast off Rte. U.S. 1 at Wequetequock. Area is due south of Wequetequock, approximately 1½ miles on Wequetequock Avenue. Large double ramp allows two launchings at a time.

Waterford—Dock Road: On Jordan Cove at Pleasure Beach approximately 2 miles south of Rte. 156.

Waterford—Niantic River: Approximately 1¼ mile northeast of Rte. 156 Bridge across Niantic River.

Westport—Saugatuck River: Off Rte. 136, approximately ¼ mile east of Saugatuck River on Underhill Parkway, under the I-95 Bridge.

The area between Race Point and The Sluiceway is known for big fish.
Roman Panek caught this 68 pounder out there while fishing with Captain
Bob Young on the Huntress.

CHAPTER 31

From The Sluiceway
To Race Point

Two weeks ago in the publisher's office three of us discussed the new bass record and the fact it came from Montauk. There were those present who thought the area between the Sluiceway and Race Point had, and still does have, a good chance at providing an 80 lb. fish.

Two years ago Bob Young and Roman Panek teamed up for one of 68 lbs. that took a trolled Gibbs plug. Others from 61 to 65 have been reported in our pages over the last eight seasons. Others I'm sure never got noticed as they were quietly shipped to market. Many, many of the regulars have tales of huge fish fought but lost.

Last fall's windy weather kept a lot of fishermen from getting out as much as they wanted. Some said this kept the record from being broken sooner. In spite of the windy weather there was still some fifties caught and some good scores late in the season by charter boats.

Besides a shot at a huge bass there's also lots of blues at times and weakfish on occasion. You can troll, jig or drift fish depending on tide or personal preference. This area is often bewildering to the newcomer because of the swift tides and amount of water.

Accompanying this story is a chart, which will help you follow along as all the material is geared to it. A good recorder is also a must. In bass fishing especially, there will be days when fish hold in tight pockets. Knowing what's where is a big help and a long study. Once you get daytime bearings, you'll have to master after dark. Practice, practice, practice.

Our first stop is the #2 buoy at the tip of the reef at Race Point. Here's a good spot for wire lining with plugs at night or jig trolling during the day. Daytime jiggers use a variety of lures but a lot do well with the JB Shovelnose or a copy thereof. Use 150' of wire. On the outgoing tide you want to troll about 50' to 75' inside the buoy. Don't go too far in or you'll thump the lower unit. One trick (practice again) is to troll uptide of the rip that forms by the buoy. When your wire is just beyond the uptide side of the dropoff, turn the boat to starboard. This will drop the jig sometimes to waiting bluefish, weakfish, maybe a bass. A northwest wind is good here. On the flood tide you want to troll about 75' outside the buoy.

Next place is the shallow water just to the east of Race Rock Light. On a chart this area is marked by a water depth of 16'. On the last two hours of the outgoing tide try this spot some night with 100' to 150' of wire and an eight inch Danny or GTS 3. Be warned it's a spooky spot on the dark moon with Race Rock flashing at you. Don't, don't go in here unless you have previous experience. This tide is tricky to gauge for newcomers. It runs from the northeast to the southwest. Make a mistake and you could end up on the stones. There's other spots around Race Rock, but those two will get you started.

One note of caution: a northwest wind is good here but don't delay if the forecast calls for freshening winds and you have to ride home back up the Sound. Once the tide turns it will be wind against the tide all the way. One night last October we dallied too long. A northwest wind was 20 and getting stiffer by the time the tide turned. The ride back to the Menunketesuck River took almost three hours instead of the normal one-and-a-half.

From Race Rock we move to the west to Valiant Rock Bell 1A. Rarely a week goes by that this spot isn't mentioned in our reports. In past years of plenty, a full moon tide provided many bass over 40 to clusters of regulars. A lot of the small boats drift fish here. One popular drift pattern is to run up-tide on the ebb to the bell. Drop the rig to the bottom and drift back to the rip. Other good drifts are ones which take you right over the peak of the shoal (water depth 18') and another which drifts over the western edge of the shoal where it drops to deeper water (water depth 27'). Try in the shallower water when the tide isn't running that hard; in the two other spots once it picks up. If all boats are clustered in one spot don't be reluctant to go somewhere else. It can get to be an awful lot like work when you are running that rip with boats coming downtide at you.

During the daylight the shoal is often the property of charter boats out making their livings. At night trollers work big plugs usually during weaker periods of tide. One favorite time frame is to troll the last hour of the flood, the slack, then the first hour of the ebb.

Next stop is the Middle Race. This is where most of the daytime bluefishing is done. On the ebb (traditionally the better tide), boats run up from the hump, drop in a variety of drift or bait rigs, then go back with the tide. Diamond jiggers also fish here. On a strong tide a couple of the better ones wait until they are at a precise spot in the drift before putting their lures down. Compact Loran C units for small boats have greatly aided such a maneuver. On days of the new moon it may run too fast here to fish the right way. On those days the better action may come the last couple hours of the ebb.

Between the Middle Race and Valiant Shoal is a section of water marked on the chart by water depths of 37' and 50'. You can drift over this spot or troll 400' to 450' of wire; not to all tastes - but possible.

Next spot is the #1 can just to the east of Little Gull. You can troll the dropoff to the east of the can (marked on the chart by the numbers 26-33) on the ebb with 275' to 300' of wire. You can also drift this section and the bottom further to the east in 50' to 80' of water. Here's one place to sneak away if Valiant gets crowded. One commercial rod and reeler once told of almost an unheard of number of fifties taken in this spot during a single tide.

Last stop on our tour is the Sluiceway. This is an underwater shelf between the eastern tip of Plum Island and the western tip of Great Gull. To be more exact the area normally fished lies between Old Silas and the shoal area marked with a 9' depth. Here's where a good number of sixties have been taken. The night the 76 lber. was caught, a steady from Sag Harbor reported he took a 66 in the Sluiceway.

If you like to troll, try by the 9' hump. On an outgoing tide a large boil can be seen on the surface. A tide line runs downstream from either edge of the rock. Run out about 90' to 110' of wire depending on lure and tide. You want to troll about 30' out from the tide line on a parallel course that takes you up into the tide. Most of our hits used to come when the console of a 19 footer was 45' to the NW or NE of the boil depending whether you came up to the west or east of the tide lines.

While some boats troll, what's left of the bass fleet drift fishes here. Two popular spots are between Old Silas and Middle Shoal Rock and about halfway between Old Silas and the 9' boil.

The ebb is the better tide but some nice fish have been taken on the flood. Try drifting to the SSE of Old Silas in the section of chart in 21' to 27' of water. On Memorial Day, 1976, Patrick and I fished here on the last part of the flood. Pat put a live mackerel over without weight because of the limited amount of tide. The mack swam straight down to a fish that took the two pound bait without so much as a burp. All of a sudden the fish had the bait and that was that. No chase on the top, nothing except one-third of the line lost from a Jigmaster before it broke off. I've always felt that was a 50 or bigger.

What's before you is just a percentage of spots available. They are some of the better known areas that should get a newcomer off in the right direction. You won't get this place down in one session; what's before you is a larger effort that depends to a great extent on how much time you are willing to put in.

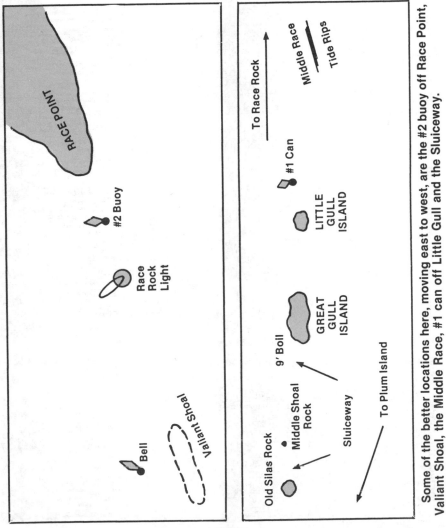

Some of the better locations here, moving east to west, are the #2 buoy off Race Point, Valiant Shoal, the Middle Race, #1 can off Little Gull and the Sluiceway.

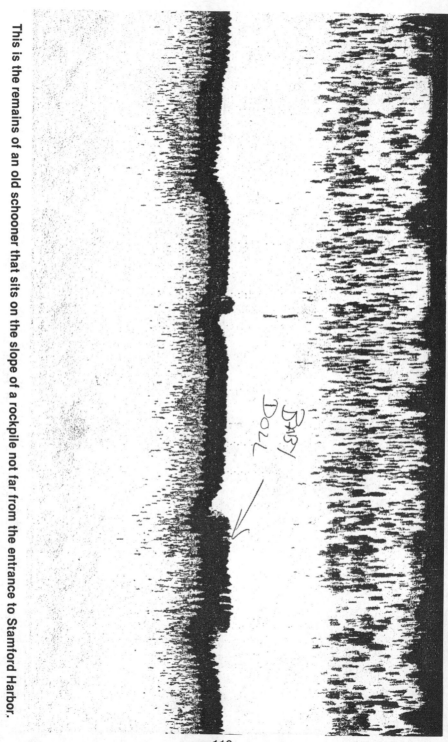

This is the remains of an old schooner that sits on the slope of a rockpile not far from the entrance to Stamford Harbor.

CHAPTER 32

Western Sound Wrecks

This week we'll turn our attention to the west, down in the end of Long Island Sound off the towns of Greenwich and Stamford, Ct. To follow along with this article get out a copy of chart 12363 which covers the west end with Loran overlay.

We started looking for wrecks in that end of the Sound after talking with Ed from Rudy's Tackle Barn in Byram. Ed said there were lots of fishable wrecks close by and sent up an old chart for us to look over. After checking the chart and other background sources, we indeed agreed it was worth a trip. Initially we set up a date with Captain Bill Herold of Billfish Charters, but with the weather the way it was this fall we kept postponing the date. Our plans were further complicated when Bill called to say he had some engine problems. At that point we were looking at next season or perhaps an alternative boat and skipper could be found. Thanks to Bill's local contacts he came up with the name Stan Schwartz who keeps his boat at the marina at 33 River Road in Greenwich. Stan is an ardent diver who loves to look for and talk about shipwrecks wherever they might be. And, what was even better, he agreed to share some of his finds and those of others with Fisherman readers.

It was a windy day back in December when we went out but Stan's 40 footer kept everybody from being blown off the water. Our first stop was the wreck of an old schooner that sits on the edge of a reef not far from the entrance to Stamford Harbor. If you run your finger along the chart approximately due south of the harbor you'll see a rock pile cleared to depths of 31 and 28 feet. On the northeast slope of the reef, leading down into deeper water, is where you'll find this wreck. We don't have any particulars on the sinking; it's another unknown ship gone to rest in New England waters.

According to Stan, the schooner is about 100 feet long with 15 foot beam. She's got a rounded stern, bow sprit and sits on her side on the bottom. The bow comes up about 10 feet while the stern is pretty flat. Stan has seen some nice blackfish on his dives to the wreck and along the rocks off to the side of the old ship. To try your hand at catching some of those tautog, head to 26856.4/43979.2 and 26856.4/43979.0.

Our next wreck is due south of Greenwich Point. Run your finger out into the Sound, stopping about a third of the way across. There you'll spot an obstruction cleared to 40 feet. In reality that obstruction is a sunken barge. Stan and his friend Ed Kostyra nicknamed this wreck the pump barge because it's got a big pump on one end which I assume filled the barge with whatever cargo it once carried. The Fisherman did a little background check on this one and found out it was 180 feet long and rises about 20 feet off the bottom at its highest point. As to fishing potential we imagine it will hold blackfish, possibly some porgies or maybe flounder in the soft bottom around the edges. To reach the pump barge go to 26872.2/43976.5.

From the pump barge run your finger to the southwest until you locate a wreck symbol cleared to 31 feet. It's approximately north of Peacock Point on the chart. This is another unknown, though Stan thinks it was some type

One of the major targets of the Western Sound wreck fisherman will be tautog.

of work boat, possibly a tug or trawler, since it has winches on deck. The housing is long gone and the hull is in two pieces on the bottom, so maybe it was the victim of a collision. The bow lies to 30 degrees, while the stern is oriented 270 degrees. In-between the two pieces is a 25 foot gap filled with debris. Overall, Stan guessed the wreck to be 90 feet with each section about 45 feet long. What's left of the hull comes up 7 feet, so you'll be able to find it with your chart machine. Stan has seen flounder around the edges and plucked some nice lobsters from the wreckage. He and Ed nicknamed this one the Baby Doll since they found a child's doll along with other souvenirs. To head to the Baby Doll in your rig, go to 26880.3/43954.8.

If there's someone out in the audience who'd like to do a little shallow water wreck fishing, this next one is for you. She sits to the west-southwest of Matinecock Point in about 25 feet of water. We're referring to the remains of the steamboat Glen Island which burned and then drifted ashore sometime in the 1800s. Stan mentioned he thought a dozen people lost their lives in that disaster. We'll guess the bones of the Glen Island provide a house for blackfish and flounder and wouldn't be surprised at all if someone with knowhow could catch a bass or two from the wreck. You'll find her at 26893.6/43937.6.

Our next wreck is due north of the Glen Island out in mid Sound. At 26893.0/43960.0, you'll find the resting spot of the scow M-35. She's listed in Notice to Mariners as sinking in 1961 approximately 1.5 miles north of Matinecock Point in roughly 55 feet of water. She comes up 7 feet off the bottom, so you should be able to spot it on your fish finder, but keep in mind all Lorans will not match up exactly; so it you arrive on the numbers but find nothing, just keep searching, the wreck is close by. Your fishing opportunities will be blackfish and porgies or perhaps some blues if the M-35 holds the bait the choppers need to survive.

From the M-35, we'll head a bit to the north to the site of yet another barge sinking, one of the dozens and dozens occurrences from New Rochelle,· N.Y. to New London, CT over the last 87 years. Stan said this wreck is a flat barge about 100 feet long that rises 10 feet. He sounded like it wasn't a very interesting dive, but fishermen might find it to their liking. To see what lives around the flat barge and just might eat half of a green crab, go out to 26895.7/43961.3.

If some of you like to run across to Long Island to fish in Hempstead Harbor, you'll want to take note of a bonus wreck Stan threw in. If the fishing in Hempstead isn't any good, you might try a stop in 40 feet of water in mid Sound approximately south-southeast of the Hens and Chickens. There sits the wreck of yet another barge, this one with coal cargo. To fish it go to 26930.5/43945.7 and 26930.6/43945.7.

If it's getting late in the day on your day off—and you keep your boat in Greenwich—you'll just have time to swing by one more wreck on your way home. South of Great Captains Island lies the wreck of the Poling Bros. #2 barge sunk sometime early in 1940. She's 120 feet long and Stan's friend Ed said he's seen some very good sized blackfish on the wreck. If you run over her the right way with your chart machine going you'll see the forward mast still sticking up from the hull. Her bow is in 70 feet of water, while the stern is slightly uphill in 60' feet. This wreck is a popular dive spot, but also hosts fishermen. The correct numbers to the last part of our story are 26894.8/43970.6.

In time, *The Fisherman* will bring you other wreck locations in the western Sound, but those will be presented by Mr. John Raguso, author of our popular Wreck Series. I spoke with John the other night and he has three tugboat wrecks, two off Norwalk and one in Huntington Bay, lined up for later this year. We might also mention that next week we'll have a story of interest to Massachusetts fishermen: the location of the barge Henry Endicott off Manomet Point on the south shore. So if you like wreck fishing just stay tuned; we've got some good stuff coming your way.

CHAPTER 33

Eastern Sound Wrecks

To follow along with this article, get chart 12354 that covers the eastern Sound with Loran overlay. On the north shore of Long Island find Mattituck Inlet, then run your finger roughly to the NNE about a third of the way across until you find a wreck symbol on the chart with the words cleared to 72 feet. That means a survey ship cleared the site for navigation to that depth. We don't have any information as to what this wreck is other than she's in 90 or so feet of water and comes up about 10 feet off the bottom. With all the barges sunk in the Sound over the last 50 years, this may indeed be the burial spot of another such craft. Because of the depth you might try this one for some summer blackfishing or check it out to see if some bluefish hold here. We marked some bait on Peter's color machine, so I imagine choppers can be caught. Please keep in mind those are guesses as to its fishing potential. I have no specific information or firsthand experience of fishing this wreck or the four others in the story. We spent the time finding them; you have to go out and see what lives there. To reach this unknown wreck, head to 14915.9 X 43946.6 and 14916.1 X 43946.5.

The next wreck is a biggie. She's located south of the western tip of Six Mile Reef. Once you find that spot on the chart, run your finger about one inch below. There you should find a wreck symbol showing the area cleared to a depth of 56 feet. Using non-copyrighted sources for background, we can tell you that's a 260 foot barge that was listed in the Notice to Mariners in 1958, so we assume that's the year she sank. On our color machine she rose 20 to 25 feet from the bottom and should be an ideal spot for blues or possibly some tautog during the summer months. She lies in 95 feet of water and is approximately 30 to 35 feet wide, so even if you make a pass across her you should be able to locate this one very easily. The 260 foot barge rests at 14902.3/43989.1 and 14902.2/43978.0.

From Six Mile Reef we'll move to the east on our chart, ending up in mid Sound, approximately south of the town of Saybrook. If you look close at the chart you'll see two wreck symbols: the northernmost one has been cleared to 79 feet, while the one about 1½ inches to the SSE has been cleared to 72 feet. Again using non-copyrighted material we can say we think those are the wrecks of the tugs Thames and Bartaria.

Of the five we found that day the Bartaria was the most difficult to find. Without a color machine I doubt if we'd have found her. The 69 foot tug sits in about 135 feet of water in an area with hard, peaky bottom. She rests on the side of a peak and without the different shading of wrecks to rocks possible with a color sounder, you'd pass right over her. She's obviously not that big a target, only coming up off the bottom about 8 feet, so look close. You might also run around checking out this whole general area as it looks like it might hold bait and blues from time to time. To fish what we think is the wreck of the Bartaria go to 14863.9/43965.9 and 14863.9/43965.5.

Next we'll head just a bit to the SSE to what we think is the wreck of the tug Thames. This wreck was listed in Notice to Mariners in 1971, so we again assume that's the year she went down. At 55 feet long and 14 feet

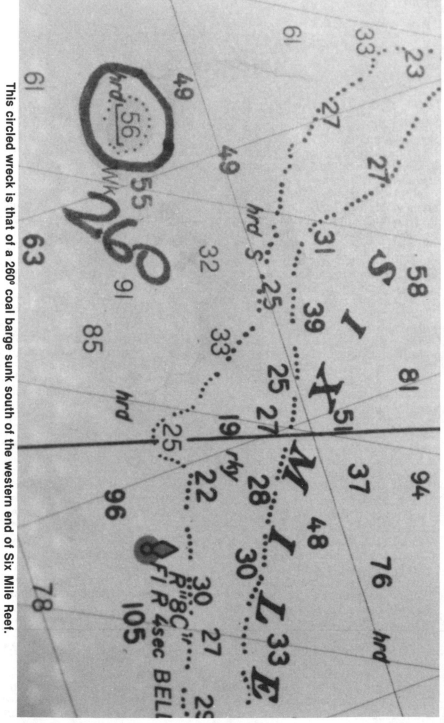

This circled wreck is that of a 260° coal barge sunk south of the western end of Six Mile Reef.

wide, this was the smallest target we searched for. She's in 128 feet of water and comes up around 10 feet. Anyone who wants to anchor on her will surely have to polish their anchoring skills especially on a running tide. We didn't mark any bait over the wreck but saw a fairly large school of something a short distance to the west.

Because this was such a relatively tiny wreck we put out a yellow marker to start a circle search. Fortunately we didn't put enough line on the float, so it started to wash to the east. At one point, after 25 fruitless minutes searching, we went over to retrieve the marker to try again. As we came up on it from the south there was the wreck of the tug directly below. It was the best mistake we made all day. To fish what we think is the wreck of the Thames, go to 14863.7/43955.6 and 14863.8/43955.6.

Our last wreck for the month of November lies about due south of the mouth of the Ct. River. In 1981 a diver identified this as a riveted, steel barge with much marine growth. Leaning once more to non-copyrighted sources, we'll take a stab and guess this is the wreck of the Cities Service's number four barge, 810 gross tons, sunk on January 24, 1936. She was listed in Coast Guard records for that year in the approximate position we found her and also listed on a Navy wreck list published in 1957. At 143 feet, this one is pretty deep for Sound fishing, but she may hold blues from time to time. To go out and see for yourself, turn the black box on for 14806.9/43970.7 and 14806.7/43970.8.

Editor's Note: Chapter 33 is a compilation of two articles. We now move on with more wrecks for the Connecticut angler who fishes the eastern end of Long Island Sound.

From updates on past wrecks we now move on to some we haven't covered before. Thanks to a tip from our source we found the wreck of the Marise, a fishing boat that at times fished out of Stonington, CT. She sits in about 75 feet of water halfway between Ram Island and East Harbor in Fisher's Island Sound. Some of the old-timers in the Mystic-Stonington area said she was a two masted dragger that had on occasion fished as far north as Nova Scotia. As late as 1965 Flip from Shaffers Boat Livery remembers her tied to a dock in Stonington.

Our source said the Marise, or what's left of it, rests on the bottom with her bow pointing upwards. The rest of it is pretty well flattened out. On a paper machine she shows up as one sharp spike coming about 10 feet off the bottom. In season she'll have blackfish on her and during the summer she's usually full of porgies. Way back when, Flip said he and others used to drift the deep water in the middle of the Sound for codfish but such fishing is mostly a memory today. To find out just what fishing opportunities the Marise holds go to 26091.6/43979.6 and 26091.7/43979.7.

From the wreck of the Marise we'll head a short distance to the western entrance to Fisher's Island Sound. There you'll find an old schooner approximately 100 feet long and rising off the bottom about 10 feet. Our source didn't have a name on this one, surmising it's been down there a long time. The swift tides that run through here keep her from sitting in like so many wrecks. Slack tide or slower tides would be an ideal time to fish the blackfish schooner as we nicknamed her since she was full of tautog.

We first fished her on 11/16/87 and can tell you from firsthand experience we caught fish on every drift, sometimes we doubled up on fish to 6 pounds. On certain drifts the schools of blackfish showed up as thin clouds just above the wreckage. She's in 50 feet of water so you might try drifting around the edges for fluke in summer, but that's just a guess on my part. To fish the blackfish schooner you will not have to run far from the state ramp at Bayberry Lane in Groton. She lies at 261116.5/43978.6 and 26116.7/43978.6. Good wreck hunting.

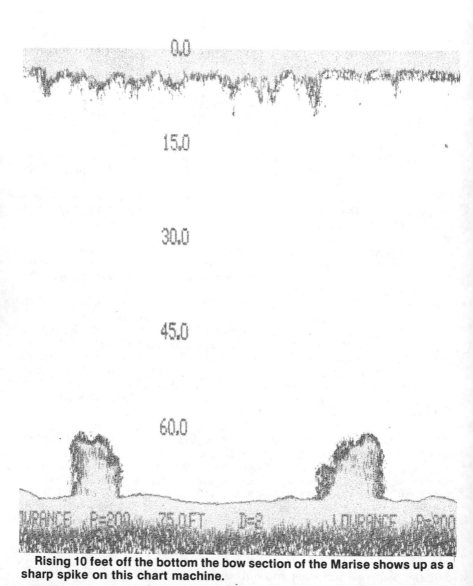

Rising 10 feet off the bottom the bow section of the Marise shows up as a sharp spike on this chart machine.

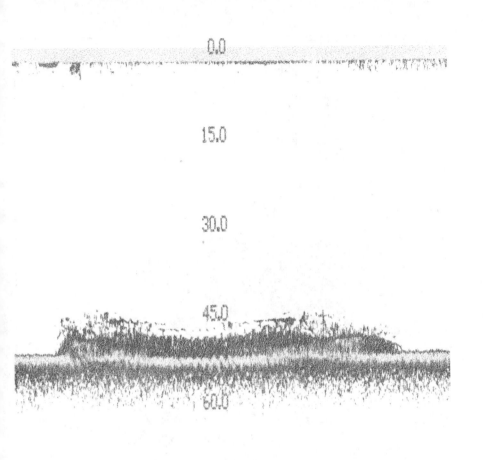

0.0

15.0

30.0

45.0

60.0

LOWRANCE P=200   75.0 FT   D=2   LOWRANCE P=

In 50 feet of water on the western end of Fisher's Island Sound you'll find the wreck of an old schooner.

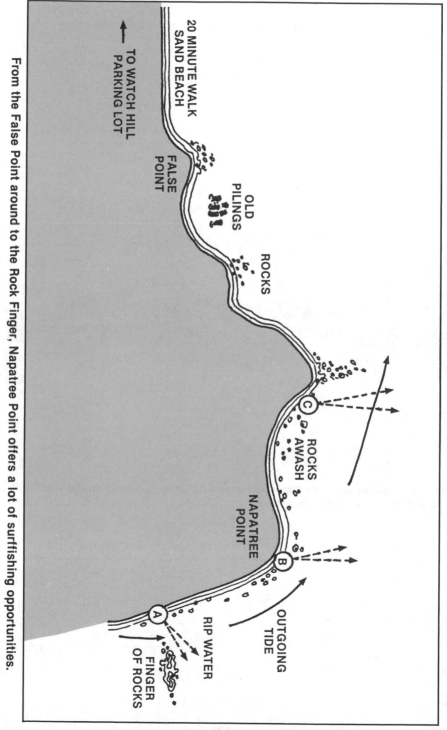

From the False Point around to the Rock Finger, Napatree Point offers a lot of surffishing opportunities.

TO WATCH HILL
PARKING LOT

20 MINUTE WALK
SAND BEACH

FALSE
POINT

OLD
PILINGS

ROCKS

C

ROCKS
AWASH

NAPATREE
POINT

B

OUTGOING
TIDE

A

RIP WATER

FINGER
OF ROCKS

CHAPTER 34

A Walk to
Napatree

Napatree Point is not Nauset. It is, however, close to home for a lot of us, and can provide sport during the fall run. Perhaps even more important, it is accessible to people with only the family car for fishing transport, if one is willing to walk a bit along a sandy beach.

This area is located to the west of fairly well known Watch Hill Light. Because of the walking distance, you are not liable to find the crowds at Napatree you might at the Light. A lot of people are just not interested in hoofing through sand. As a result, you can often fish in peace—all night long if you wish.

To reach here, get off I-95 at the exit for Pawcatuck-North Stonington. Take a right at the bottom of the ramp and then follow this road all the way through Pawcatuck, into the Town of Westerly. Once in town get on Beach St. and stay with it right into Watch Hill. Watch Hill is made up of mainly large houses and small shops. You can park your car at the parking lot near a cluster of such shops near the Watch Hill Yacht Club. In the past the police never bothered us, particularly during the fall when tourists are gone. I'm sure most of you are well aware of the problems of access in these parts. If you go fishing, by all means use your head; don't make a lot of noise, or throw trash about.

Once you get out of your car, walk along the stone wall bordering the harbor next to the beach club. About an eighth of a mile down you'll see a fence at a 90° angle to the wall. There's room enough to pass around the fence. Continue walking along the path in the sand, up and over the dunes till you get to the beach. Napatree Point is off to the west. It's about a 20 minute walk.

Toward the end of your walking you'll see some old pilings up ahead along the beach. Just before the pilings, if you look a little closer, you'll see a slight point in the beach. Seaward of this are rocks and bits of man made rubble I assume was dumped there after the '38 hurricane. Seas build up around this point, with some nice white water at times and drop offs on the east and west side. This spot is always worth a cast or two, especially if there's a decent amount of water over the point. Don't spend the whole night here. If you don't get a bump or two in 10 to 15 minutes, move on.

The best tide to fish Napatree is open to question. My favorite has always been the drop. In going around to clubs, and at shows here in our office, I've heard from a noticeable number of people who've done well here on the incoming. The best thing to say might be go fishing when you have the time. From my own standpoint, I always fished Watch Hill on the incoming, then gone here once it dropped.

Anyway, after clearing the false point go past the old pilings and onto a beach made up of rocks, not sand. Not too far along the rock beach, is a very haphazard finger of rocks sticking out into the surf. It's probably better labeled as a sprawl of rocks that you can get to the tip of once the tide drops down a bit. The outgoing tide will sweep by you heading from roughly the NW to the SE. By positioning oneself somewhere near the circled "C" in

This pair of 17 pound blues were caught on a swimming plug one night in early November.

the diagram, you can work a plug or eel back along those rocks. The force of the dropping tide will really bring out the action in a plug. Nothing says you can't use eels here, either live or rigged, except maybe some blues which will likely be the mainstay of your catch.

From this spot you walk further to the east along a section of shore paved with mussel shells. Go past them until you reach a point where the shore bends around to the north. At that point, you'll see the start of very large boulders piled up right on the beach. Prior to this area, boulders were in the water, but not right up on dry land. This spot is marked with a circled "B". Rocks here open up a bit permitting someone to walk out on them to cast into the tide without too much distance separating fisherman from fish.

Next stop on our walking tour is around the bend from B. If you look off the NW you'll see a finger of rocks running in a straight line from east to west. This finger does not extend all the way to the shore. A gap of about 200 to 250 feet separates the two. On a dropping tide, water flowing out of the Pawcatuck River flows through this gap and causes a tide rip to the south. The rip will really be pronounced if you get a SW wind blowing against the tide. When the water is clean, and those conditions prevail, chances for success are very, very good in spot A.

Unfortunately 1982 is not 1972. Bass are not gone by any means, but your chances are not all that good. Still, hope springs from a soul who has chosen the beach as his fishing platform. You just might hit a nice bass but I'd bet a steaming cup of coffee that for every bass you find, you have to go through a bunch of blues. In September through early October, weakfish might be found in the rip. A chance at a trophy bluefish is there, particularly on nights with swifter tides.

Plugs that work here are the medium sized Danny topwater swimmer or the old reliable Atom Jr. Don't get carried away with popping plugs. Swimmers will catch better, particularly if it's a bass you are looking for. If the wind prevents a suitable toss, there's always the Gibbs bottle plugs, in two, possibly three ounce size. Droppers work up ahead of your plugs, but blues will cut you off if the dropper is rigged with mono. Other plugs at home here are the seven inch plastic swimmers though I wouldn't fish a loaded Red-Fin. It's liable to run too deep and get hung up.

Lines for either spinning or conventional should be on the heavy side as there's not too much chance of not having your line brush up against a rock sooner or later. For spinning try 17 or 20 pound test while 30 pound mono is good for conventional. One last item you'll need is a rope for carrying fish, and some stamina. Five blues from 10 to 17 pounds average out to about 14 pounds if two of the fish weighed 17, and another was just over 15. If you want to get those back to the folks at home, you'll be in for a hefty tote. Hint: drag them along the sand with a long rope. I'll bet you stop at least three times for air before you reach your car.

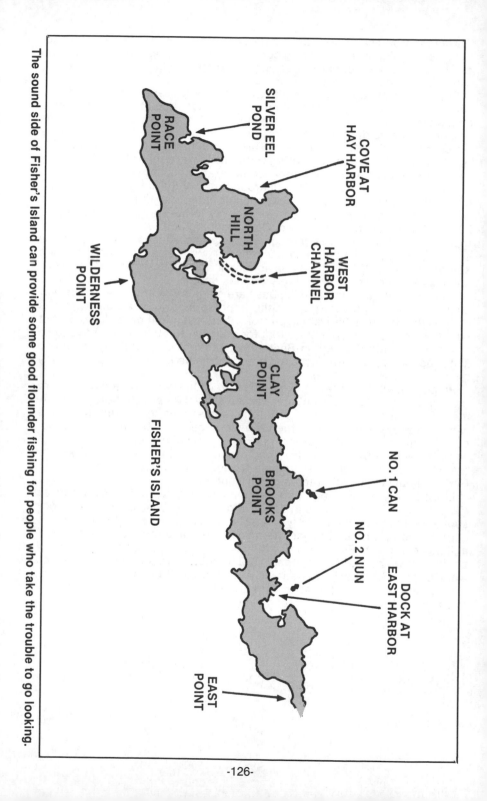

The sound side of Fisher's Island can provide some good flounder fishing for people who take the trouble to go looking.

CHAPTER 35

Flounders
of Fishers

Our fishing reports usually prompt all kinds of letters and/or inquiries at our office. A couple of those letters were from people who wanted more information of where to fish for flounder on the north side of Fisher's Island. This isn't Quincy, numbers-wise, but it usually has larger flounder, and it's close to home for a lot of our readers.

I've fished some over here, particularly around Thanksgiving after most bass departed. But, to get a good firsthand impression from somebody who's fished here all his life, we turned to Mr. Luciano Bellastrini. To a lot of you who rent boats from Shaffer's Boat Livery in Mystic, CT, Mr. Bellastrini is better known as Flip. Flip, from atop a stool behind the counter at Schaffer's, agreed to part with a few pointers.

Fishing should be going good about now, though keep in mind, the fishing here hasn't been as good the last couple years as it was in the past. Be that as it may, a couple people stand a fair chance of taking a couple dozen nice flounder in a day's fishing.

Our first stop on our short tour will be down the east end of the Island. From there we will work our way to the west. Way up inside East Harbor you'll see a dock. Fishing not far off this dock early in the year can be very productive. Later on (just about now), it's best to fish outside the harbor. Flip likes to line up the #1 can off Brooks Point with the North Dumpling. This area is doubly productive if you fish it just after one of the islanders pulls his pots. It has a chumming effect on the fish that really can perk things up.

Actually flounder can be caught anywhere between the #1 can and the #2E nun to the east in about 18 to 20 feet of water. Sometimes, not always, flounder fishing will last through the summer. Other years, the fishing stops somewhere in July. It will start up again, depending on the weather, sometime in the fall.

Another spot worth fishing is in the channel, or just outside of it leading into West Harbor. One thing to keep in mind, is if you fish East Harbor, and the flood tide goes slack, you can run over here and still have fishable tide. The reverse is true on the ebb. In his days as a commercial bluefisherman (back in the 30s), Flip and his father used to get ten hours fishing out of a single tide between Cerberus Shoal and the Bloody Grounds.

Last place Flip suggested was over around Hay Harbor. There's a small cove there just behind North Hill. It's fairly rocky in that general area, so you stand a chance at picking up a blackfish as well as a flat. For that reason, Flip suggested a #6 Chestertown.

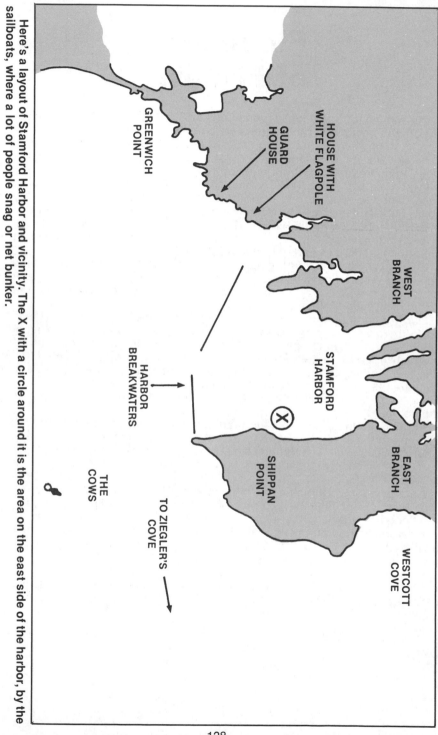

Here's a layout of Stamford Harbor and vicinity. The X with a circle around it is the area on the east side of the harbor, by the sailboats, where a lot of people snag or net bunker.

HOUSE WITH WHITE FLAGPOLE

GUARD HOUSE

GREENWICH POINT

WEST BRANCH

STAMFORD HARBOR

HARBOR BREAKWATERS

EAST BRANCH

SHIPPAN POINT

THE COWS

TO ZIEGLER'S COVE

WESTCOTT COVE

CHAPTER 36

Stamford Harbor For Bass

By the time the sun was up we had all our bait and were on our way across Stamford Harbor bound for a morning of bass fishing. Before the trip was over, two local hiliners generously parted with plenty of solid info on where to find bass around this town.

The two are Pat Charillo, formerly of Pat's Marina, who is a second generation Stamford fisherman, resident and tackle dealer. The other was Fred Bova, a fellow who has taken thousands of jumbo fish in the area. Between the two of them was many, many years experience riding in the one boat.

We cleared Pat's place about 4:35 AM or so, then headed down the West Branch of the harbor. The bunker supply wasn't far, just around the sailboats on the east shore of the harbor. A few blues had the bait rousted about by the time we arrived, but there was more than enough to go around. Fred uses a 50 foot section of gill net, rather than snagging. It's much quicker. In two sets we had 30 to 40 bait. Note: he uses 2½ inch mesh on his net. He feels the adult bunker will just get their noses up in there, but won't become fully gilled. As such, they are easier to pop out of the net. Some went into the Sea Craft's live well, while others went into a five gallon bucket, to be used for chunk bait.

Our first stop was on the western side of the harbor, just off a shorefront house with a white flagpole out front. If the house owner likes surf fishing, he has it made. We were right in his backyard. We can't give the range, but if you look on a chart you'll see the reef that runs out from the house. You want to anchor up close to the rocks (underwater at high tide) on the eastern side of the reef.

This spot is best from 1½ hours before to 1½ hours after high water. Beyond that point, you can forget about the flagpole, said Fred. He likes to anchor up in the shallow water. On two rods he puts out a live bunker on one, and on another a fresh juicy chunk. He feels the lazy, jumbo bass might play with the live bait a couple times, but usually end up eating the easy-to-get chunk. He gave me the feeling the live one is used a lot of times just as an attractor.

While the two bait rods are in the water, Fred further increases his chances by picking up a light spinning stick and plugging with a ¾ ounce Creek Chub popper. Even if he doesn't get any hits Fred felt the plugging wasn't wasted as the topwater's noise also draws fish to the baits. Or, if there's only school fish around that trip they will readily take the small plug. The day before we fished, Fred had seven legal bass in one morning thanks to the plugging.

During the course of our 1½ hours' stay in front of the flagpole, we took a bass just under 20 on the chunk, had a fish around 30 swirl under one of the live ones plus five or so bunkers were chopped in half. Certainly no shortage of life around that reef that day. To fish the bunkers, both live and chunked, Fred uses 8/0 O'Shaughnessy's tied directly to 50 pound mono on a couple boat rods wih Jigmaster reels. He does not use any leader. If blues cut him off, it doesn't really matter as he's mainly looking for bass.

Bass action at the flagpole dried up near the top of the tide, so off we went, just a little further to the west. There's a small green building just at the head of the swimming beach on the way out to the tip of Greenwich Point. That's the guardhouse. If you'll check a chart once more you will see that spot, like the flagpole, has a boulder-strewn bottom, perfect place for bass to come looking for breakfast. Here we had a fish swirl three times under the popper, but didn't hit. Fred felt that fish had just so much bait in it he wasn't really that hungry. This area had loads and loads of bait. However, that day the guardhouse didn't provide any more, except a couple rolls under the last couple live ones. Seeing how the tide was due to change, it was time once more to move.

Over we went past Smith Reef, to the east of Long Neck Point in Darien. People who live here know this as Ziegler's Cove. We fished just outside the steps leading down to the water. That day a perfect range was lining the Egret up with the steps. Since the Egret moved, you'll have to poke about a bit, but it's there. Fred likes this spot just as the tide turns to go out. It was here that he took the seven small fish the day before.

At Ziegler's Cove, though, our day ended. The summer sun was climbing higher and the water started to take on that glassy look that usually spells the end of the bass action for that morning. With that, we'll have to take our leave of Fred though you can bet he was out off the flagpole the next morning and the next and the next. That's the reason Fred usually ends up the day with a bass or so.

CHAPTER 37

Bunker & Blues

Making a twenty-five minute movie for clubs sometimes takes a bit of doing. Things like the weather play ups and downs on you. The day before you arrive, it's beautiful. The very next morning a front comes through affecting fish in the process. Throw in the curse of the camera (said curse causing every fish in a fifty mile radius to scram) and it sometimes takes a year to complete the project.

That's about the way it went. Last September, Ted Keatley agreed to take me out into Stamford Harbor to shoot scenes of blues herding bunker in the upper reaches of the West Branch. Fish were thick two days before I got there. By Friday though, not a flip nor swirl were evident. That night a front went through dumping rain, rain, rain on our early morning efforts to get bait. The rest of the day was cold northeast that produced little but conviction in Ted plus a chill in the cameraman. Ted was convinced cameras and bluefishing, his bluefishing, did not mix.

Time heals though. By September, 1983, Ted again agreed to tempt fate. Bunker with large blues right behind them had been in and out around the Stamford breakwalls. Getting bait hadn't been a problem; things looked good.

It was a bright, clear morning as we motored outside the sailboats on the east side of the harbor. With the glass smooth water you can easily tell there wasn't a bunker to be seen. We went all the way up into the west branch, then over to the east section, finally back to the sailboats. Guess who was thinking what about this time? I was getting ready to volunteer to be left atop a piling, afterwhich I'd hitch a ride back home.

Ted is a man of preparation, just in case. He'd checked with his sources prior to the camera jinx arriving on his doorstep. The day before blues rushed a ton of bunker in Greenwich Cove right on the high water. Around Todd's Point we went, past a couple boats anchored up chunking. Who says it didn't pay to light two thousand candles in a nearby church the day before the trip? Up in the cove we found more bunker than the U.S. budget has red ink.

In twenty minutes snagging, Ted and his young fishing partner Dave had enough bait to round out the movie. Last year we had some footage but it was mainly leaden clouds, cold anglers and almost nonexistent bluefishing. That day was warm and we were about to complete our project.

To exorcise the curse Ted had aboard his 20' Shamrock he decided to fish his pet spot, a place reserved when things get tough in around the harbor. Tough might mean lots of blues but too many weekend warriors. The location is an unmarked reef about a mile to the SSE of the bell on the outside of the Cows. Did I say mile? It might be more, then again, a bit less. It's out there though, a high section that comes up to forty-one feet.

Ted likes to hit this place just as the current is easing down. He definitely doesn't like it on a hard running tide. Once anchored on the right ranges he'll go to work with live bunker. He will fish chunks too but favors the live ones more than anything.

To keep bunker alive, Ted uses two plastic garbage barrels; one fits inside the other. When the boat is moving a fast water pickup forces water up into both barrels. A three inch hose acts as the overflow which drains over

The first three places we looked for bait were barren. We checked the West Branch, the the East Branch and back around the sailboat moorings. A ride over to Greenwich Cove was necessary to get bait.

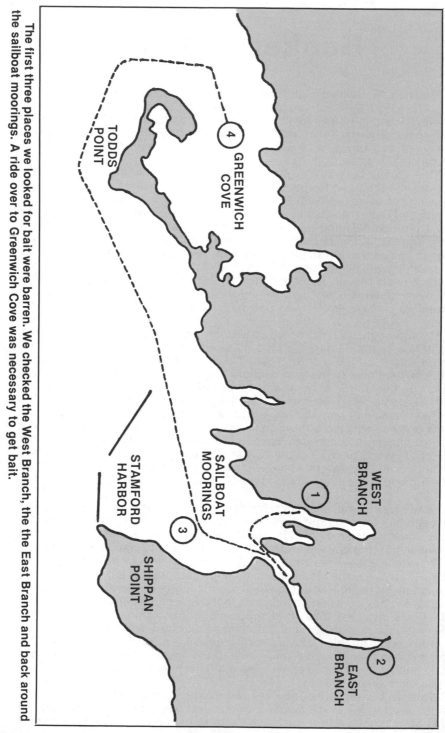

Ted Keatley, shown here, has since decided the New England winters are too harsh and retired to Florida. Photo by Art Glowka.

the gunwale. When the Shamrock stops, Ted takes out the inside barrel, with holes cut in the sides, and places it in the water next to the boat (barrel is tied off to the handrail). His reasoning behind the two containers is he doesn't like to run a bait pump. The extra barrel keeps his bunker healthy without a drain on the battery.

To fish the large baits, Ted rigs up two 7/0 Sproat hooks in tandem on a wire line. About a twelve inch section of leader is used on the first hook. One end is crimped into the eye of the hook while a loop is formed in the other end by crimping the wire back on to itself. The leader of the second hook is crimped around the bend of the first. The other end of this second piece of leader is then crimped to the eye of the second hook. A 2 to 3 inch piece of wire is fine for this back hook.

The first hook goes into the bunker behind the dorsal fin. The second goes around the tail, held in place by a small rubber band. The hook is flush against the bunker but doesn't go into the flesh. To weigh the bunker down, Ted uses drails of various sizes. the weights are attached to the loop in the leader with sturdy duo lock snaps. After that you lower the bait to the bottom to await results.

Ted likes to fish four rods. To get things moving in the right direction Ted chums with pieces of frozen bunker. About fifteen minutes after the first chum was over we had our first hit. Ted set up to miss what we found out a short time later were small fish. If large blues are about you don't miss many with the two hook setup. That trip we caught eight from four to seven pounds. On trips prior to the camera adventure all of the fish were over ten pounds. Naturally the size dropped off when you know who showed up. Ted's outside reef is capable of producing blues of monster size. Last year Stamford resident Art Glowka nailed a twenty-one pounder there which was heavy enough to take first prize in the bluefish division of the Halloween Yacht Club Tournament.

Thank God, we did get our movie. It took a year between takes but things finally fell into place. Ted, back on land, savored an after-the-trip ice cream cone. He'd taken Curse and his camera out and actually caught fish. Our trip probably won't rate a mention in the I.G.F.A. Yearbook but it was a milestone in the fishing career of Mr. Ted Keatley.

CHAPTER 38

Some Humor
How to Fib Good

There you are, just returned from a much-publicized fishing trip. Your wife has six people—including grandmom—ready to clean all your catch. Naturally, the first question when they see you is, how did you make out?

Or, you make your first appearance in the office or locker room after returning from your vacation. Prior to this, you've told everyone how many fish you were going to rake in. Maybe you went so far as to take orders for fillets. Again, the first response when they see you is how many?

Now if you've got the cat in the bag, no problem. However, there are those times when you choose the wrong ocean. Then what do you do? Honest, truthful fishermen own up to defeat; the remaining 99.9% of us start fibbing. Here's a few pointers.

Never start out with "we didn't get a thing." Worst thing you can do; the situation will deteriorate from there. If sizeable money was expended, your wife might not let you go again if it's a clear-cut case of no meat on the table. Instead say, "Well, we didn't make out so good." Add quickly to that the tide was against the wind with a big sea running. Right there you've built two doors to make your escape.

Lets take door number one. If the person presses you for an exact count of how many is not so good, say you were not really sure since partner Harry took 'em all with him. It helps if Harry lives in Minnesota and is not available for comment. In reality Harry didn't take any since there were none to take.

From this point, go right into door number two. You've told the inquirer what you did, now tell him why fishing wasn't "so good." "Big sea up, lots of tide against the wind"; that sentence always sounds like you know what you're talking about. Be forewarned if you went to Billings Lake about using the latter. Someone is just liable to innocently state he didn't know there was a rise and fall of tide in Billings. At that point, you are on your own.

On difficult days try blaming the fog. Say you couldn't get out. "Couldn't see two feet in front of me"; that's a classic that is well respected by non-fishermen waiting to see all the fish you told them you would catch. "Next week for sure" is an old faithful that always props up the fog part. Never forget to remind the person who is NOT going to eat fish tonight that conditions are always different down by the water. This is just in case your fib is being told under a beautiful mantle of blue with nary a cloud in any direction.

No matter how good you are at avoiding the awful truth, you will always run into somebody who has the nerve to say, "Ah, I don't believe a word you say." The best move is to offer proof. One of the best proofs is a fish. Simply leave a fish on ice from the last trip. Presto - instant proof! The rest are with Harry. Remember door number one. Of course, make sure you remember the proof on ice, otherwise your story will literally sink if you wait too long.

The above fibs are "tried and trues" that have withstood the test of time. For those wanting something a little newer—try this one. Grandmom went fishing with you. Naturally, since grandmom is 93, she's not as snappy as a mere fifty years back. Consequently, you didn't get many fish because grandmom was a little slow when it came to snapping bucktails on 300 feet of wire line. I dare anyone to tell you differently.

-135-

Surfcasters can always say they donated their fish to somebody from Texas Instruments who was doing a study on bass. You just happened to bump into this fellow on a night trip to a lonely beach. Everybody has heard of eccentric professors, right? They are just as believable as slow grandmoms. Tell whoever the doubter is to call a certain number, at a certain time to verify your story. Make sure the bartender turns down the TV set when he goes to answer the phone as you instructed him to do.

Probably the easiest way out of this perplexing problem is changing your status from a non-catching to a catching fisherman. The best way to go about that little chore is enjoyable. To do away with little fibs, to have fish in the box more often, you have to roll up your sleeves and go to work learning about fishing. The best way to do that is on the job training. So for the sake of a more honest world, it is your duty to get out on the water more often. And that, my friend, I wouldn't lie to you about.

Keeping a Nodder Awake

My friend, Charlie, is the type of person who seems to have a turbine inside of him. He just keeps going and going, long after people like me need a battery charger. Charlie can stay up all night, then troll bunker hour after hour in a hot July sun. At the end of the trip, he can still drive home.

His partner, on the other hand, is nodding even before they pull away from the ramp on the trip home. Since a lot of fishermen like Charlie have partners like me, I thought it might be a public service to offer suggestions on how to get a nodder awake.

After clearing the ramp, Charlie usually makes a couple stabs at conversation, usually to no avail. His next stab is in the ribs. This brings signs of life from the other occupant of the cab of the pickup. Charlie's partner opens his eyes long enough to see the look on Charlie's face, which says why don't you do something besides fall asleep. So I do. I get out Charlie's thermos, pour myself a cup of Charlie's coffee, swallow Charlie's coffee, then rest my eyes after doing something.

Once that plan has failed, try turning the stereo up full blast. The tape with the sound track from the movie "Rocky" is a wise choice. Be on the lookout for the height of audacity; your partner reaching over to turn down a stereo that doesn't belong to him. Here you should politely whisper to your partner if he does that again, you will tear off his right arm and use it to break all the fingers on his left hand.

If your partner is a real in-depth nodder, even the stereo might not work. Nodders are tough when it comes to sleeping on the way home. Of course, it might have been your tone of voice when you mentioned turning down the stereo. Try a megaphone placed one-quarter inch from his left ear. I can't really recommend any place to get a good buy on a megaphone, though you might try Charlie. At times, I think he will try anything short of manslaughter to keep me awake.

The next move might be pulling into a Howard Johnson's. Have your partner get out to get some coffee. However, don't be upset if he forgets to get you a cup, or he comes back with your coffee chock-full of pure cane sugar when you take only Sweet and Low. Remember, the nodder is half asleep to begin with. If the nodder isn't too swift when he's awake, the whole project could be a disaster when a person is a small yawn away from closing his eyes.

Here's a plan some say is justified when dealing with such a serious problem as a sleepy fishing partner. Get a bunker (I told you you were going to like this one) and place it a short distance from the nodder's nose. It definitely helps if the bait is well sunburned. The aroma is enough to wake anything short of a mummy.

If the bunker bit doesn't produce, here is a last resort. Keep an eye out as you go along the road. When you see the right one, pull in. Make sure the place is nice looking and well kept. You wouldn't want anything less for a partner of yours. Take him out of the vehicle. At this point, either drag him along by the feet or arms. Rest him gently against one of the stones and, for goodness sake, leave him somewhere where someone will spot him. Some other party will take it from there. One last word of caution: as you drive out the main gate of the cemetery, look both ways before heading out on the road. You don't want to get into an accident for the sake of your partner. If he didn't respond to the bunker treatment, he's not going to respond. He died in his sleep!

Choosing and Maintaining A Fishing Partner

There is probably nothing so precious to a fisherman as his steady fishing partner. The companion of once a week doesn't count here. We are talking about the person you call first when you hear about a steady pile of fish someplace. That's the one who makes or breaks the trip.

If you don't have a steady fishing partner, here's some tips for choosing someone for this great honor. Fishing partners usually get along on a compensating basis. If one always forgets coffee because he is single, the other always remembers because he is married. If one can't find the bass at night because his glasses are blurred with spray, then the other probably eats a lot of carrots and has uncorrected 20/20 in each eye. If one thinks tide is something to wash clothes with, the other has the highs and lows of every day memorized for a six-month period.

If one shows up at the dock without a single hook, the other needs four trips just for different color bucktails. If one, shall we say, exaggerates, the other understates. Taking an average would provide an accurate score.

With the need for compensation in mind, you will probably have to search long and hard for the right candidate. It is entirely feasible to make twenty-five different trips with different people and not have one meet the stringent requirements. Say you have a beach buggy with a narrow, eight foot space set aside for sleeping. If you are six feet tall, that means you need a fishing partner who can't be over twenty-four inches high. See what I mean—good fishing partners are tough to come by.

You may have to overlook some minor flaws in return for other pressing considerations. Say you make $10,000 a year. You have this burning desire to catch a swordfish. Swords are tough to come by casting from the beach. Consequently, even if a prospective person snores in his sleep, votes Republican while you are a devout Democrat, loves champagne while you guzzle Budweiser, constantly plays Beethoven while you groove on the Texas Trio, you will probably have to overlook his flaws if he owns a forty-two foot Sportfisherman. In the interest of honesty, fair play and catching a sword, tell the guy how much you enjoy his champagne.

Other considerations pop into view at certain times of the year. If you are a surfman who has been watching fish breaking just out of reach, if might be a good idea to look for a partner around the docks or launch ramps.

If you've got a galley in your twenty-six footer, maybe you ought to reconsider that fisherperson who doesn't quite duplicate Farah Fawcett. She might not look that good, but oh, what she can't do with fresh flounder and home fries. A lot of factors must be considered in such a delicate selection for a fishing partner.

If you do come upon a lady fair who can cook like sixty, fish like Joe Brooks and looks like Raquel Welch—watch out. The small matter of your wife might have to be taken into consideration. She might frown on your setting sail with a "buddy" clad in a bikini.

At this point in the story, my friend Patrick called. As usual, Patrick didn't want to discuss the movement of goods and services. He was interested in the flow of tides, bait and bass. While I had a hold on Patrick's ear, I asked him about choosing a fishing partner. His replies:

1. Finding a good fishing partner is tougher than locating a girl friend.

2. If you are left-handed, it helps if your partner is right-handed, especially if you both like to fish off the same rock.

3. Fishing partners should never let their wives communicate. That could be tough. Editor's Note: what happens if you told the old lady you were taking so-and-so's kids to the circus, when in reality you and so-and-so went fluke fishing?

4. Partners should use different lures. Editor's Note: Patrick's got a good point here. If you've bought a lure that's either terrific or an unmitigated turkey, give it to your partner. If he goes fishless five trips in a row, you know it's no good. At this point you can move to the forefront via the compensating principle: tell your partner "tough luck" about his poor luck. Don't by any means feel sad. After all, your partner was just doing his job.

Once you get a good partner, it wouldn't hurt to make sure he carries his end of the load. Let him clean and cook the fish, then you pitch in to eat them. After you dock the boat for him, let him clean the boat for you. If you buy the coffee, let him get the flat of worms. If he squawks, remind him he was hand-picked for the job. That's a hefty honor. Tell him to watch his step or he'll blow a good thing.

Every once in awhile, it doesn't hurt to give the person a loyalty test of some sort. Instead of you telling your wife you are going fishing for the fourth straight evening, have your partner do it. That isn't cowardice on your part. No, sir. You are just doing it to ensure you get the chance to take your partner fishing.

Tell him when he calls your wife that you won't take no for an answer. Folks always look up to other folks who stand on their beliefs. And I'll bet you strongly believe you don't want to talk to your wife about going fishing once more.

As the partnership grows older, always keep your friend tuned in on necessary adjustments. Say you decide to go out all day instead of just one tide. This calls for notification by you to your partner for his providing a bigger lunch, more gas money, a larger supply of bait and a better set of excuses. That bit about recurring dental problems is wearing thin. The boss is also giving the one on the weekly civil defense drills a little closer scrutiny.

If possible, have your partner join the National Guard. When he shows up at work in his uniform, the boss will believe you and he are off to defend the country. Get the boss in the habit of the need for a weekly or semi-weekly defense posture. Whatever you do, don't be afraid to bring up the subject to your partner. Excuses, like tires, only last so long.

In the end, you will be glad you were selective in the beginning. Don't settle for less than a good person for the position. Get somebody honest to a fault, who knows fishing from apples to zebras, who will do his utmost to make every trip a success, who won't holler when things go wrong and who shows promise at thinking up excuses. When you find such a person, treat him like a brother and please don't charge him below minimum wage for the heavy task he's about to undertake.

T.A.T. is Coming!!

Most of the fishing for fish is over for the 1978 season; however, there's an important event necessary to the success of the 1979 season that is fast approaching. Some folks call this event Christmas; others label it tackle acquisition time, or TAT for short. If you do well at TAT, you'll have all the goodies you need to snag, break up or cast off next year.

The smart angler starts prepping the folks at home right after Thanksgiving. That's when thoughts turn to shopping. Yes, December 25 is approaching.

Say that 4/0 is not what it used to be. The ol' gears have cranked in one too many blues. How do you drop the hint? Well, you could leave the reel right by the better half's breakfast plate - no doubt she'll inquire about a reel on the kitchen table. Tell her you were up until all hours fixing the thing, but had no luck. However, you will keep trying seeing as how you don't want to spend any of your money on tackle with Christmas coming up and all. Once she has the reel she can take it to a tackle store, item in hand. No offense to any fisherperson, but some wives don't know a 4/0 from an 0/4. She can go in and say, "I want one of these."

Don't let grandmom off the hook. Mine is eighty-six, yet she gets a little nudge at this time of year. Drop off a set of foul weather gear that needs mending. Seeing how the average grandmom can't mend rubber, she might think about getting you a new set. Keep an eye peeled for an energetic grandmom doing her grandson a big favor by hand-stitching a nice, new corduroy patch on your Helly Hansens. Tough luck when it starts to rain.

How are you fixed for plugs? Not so good, you say? Let's look around and see who we can tap for TAT purposes for this category. Do you car pool to work in your car? If that's the case, leave some lures on the back seat (minus hooks, of course). When Harry or Joe or Sam goes to sit down, bring him up short. Hopefully, someone will pick up the conversation from there. Tell him you've been looking all around for that particular lure, but can't seem to find any. You might want to try this with three or four buddies in the car. The "buddy" who comes up dry come Christmas should be put in the coldest part of the car the first trip back to work after the holidays.

Little ones running in and out of the house? Bet they'd love to get Daddy somethin' nice for Christmas. Let's kill two birds with one stone. Put some mono on the floor. When the little darlin's go screamin' through Saturday afternoon, stop them before they get caught up in it. First you "lecture" them on running through the house and keeping quiet just before the football game. Second, you might mention how they just about messed up Daddy's only fishing line. Don't do as one parent suggested. The poor man said he was going to strangle the little ... with the line, then go get some new stuff. Needless to say, we here at *The Fisherman* would never recommend anything that drastic. Further, we would never run a story dealing with the proper way to strangle your kids with mono if they make too much noise. The fact that it's only the first half of a beautiful rainy Saturday is not a mitigating circumstance.

When all else fails, you must take matters into your own hands. If TAT time looks like a bummer, do what a friend of mine did. He got his wife just what she always wanted: a brand new nineteen foot Aquasport, complete with bait system and chart machine. That's what you call the Christmas Spirit.

Last, I'll bet grandmom would really appreciate a subscription to *The New England Fisherman.* Don't get worked up if grandmom can't see so well—she'll love ya for it. Heck, my grandmother reads *The Fisherman* all the time.

Travels With Wheezer

Wheezer is my fishing car, something we all have, but I'll bet or hope you don't ever own anything like Wheezer. She's a white, two-door, compact model; she's a poor misfit whose creators probably put the finishing touches on her on the Monday morning after New Year's Eve; she's a disaster waiting to take someone fishing; she's an all pro lemon, complete with roof rack for fishing poles.

In time, I'll take Wheezer out to a deserted field somewhere near a good striper beach and shoot it, then leave it for the sea gulls to crap on. Or perhaps I'll donate Wheezer to the Sport Fishing Fund as an artificial reef, but the cod and tautog would give it back, as she'd somehow cause problems for them. If anyone out there in the audience owns a machine like Wheezer, read on, for misery may take comfort in numbers.

This past summer *The Fisherman* ran a story about a trip from Gloucester out to the mid-reach of Georges Bank to a spot called Cultivator Shoal. What we didn't write about until now was on the way home Wheezer rose to the occasion by performing something more than her normal breakdowns. Just north of the I-93 turnoff to Lowell, Ma., from Interstate 95, Wheezer decided to stop running. One minute she was doing 55 to 60 MPH, the next second, zippo. Luckily the outside lane was empty, so I coasted to a stop off the shoulder. Ever come off a three-day fishing trip, half tired, with three hours driving ahead of you, to find it's going to be a l-o-n-g night thanks to one more sleight of hand from your car?

The reason for the breakdown was a timing chain let go, which cost $280 to repair at the local dealer where I got Wheezer; the same dealer will not be getting a Christmas card this season. To arrive at the dealer it cost $345 for towing from Wakefield, MA. to Mystic, CT. It was either that or wait around until the next morning, something not possible since I had appointments in the office the next day.

I can remember climbing in Wheezer one cold morning soon after the warranty ran out to find both the clock and rear window defroster didn't work. Over—once more—at the dealer, the mechanic ($32/hour) politely explained how both the clock and defroster were on the same wire, so that's why they went out together. I took small comfort in that as I paid the bill.

This past summer we returned via Wheezer from a day of yellowfin tuna fishing on a hot, hot afternoon. If you got three guesses as to which part would stop on such a day, what would you say? The air conditioner, of course. That meant—once more— going back to the dealer to hear it was a hose that let go and it would need a back order. I, of course, should return once the part arrived and, of course, pay for the first visit. On my second visit they installed the hose after, of course, paying for the second visit. The A/C worked fine for about 1½ days; it stopped this time about the time Wheezer passed the Mass Pike cutoff off I-95, heading south. From there back to Westerly, RI, it blew a steady, consistent, balmy stream of hot air.

Wheezer doesn't always head north on I-95 to go fishing; at times she's gone down and back to Key West. On her first two attempts, she behaved herself, but on the third time, she came home needing front end struts. Those cost $200 plus installation. I should have taken the burning gas station in Georgia as a sign Wheezer would assert herself on the way home. Burning station? On the way down we stopped for gas, in the middle of a teeming rain, somewhere in the Peach State. As Wheezer came off the exit ramp, there right out the front window, looking like something out of the battle scenes from Platoon was a Shell Station completely ablaze. Yellow flames licked the roof of the office, while ominous pink jobbies danced about the bays. With the sirens of the local engine company coming up the road, I figured it might be wise to get fuel in another location.

While that was a fiery moment in Wheezer's 62,000 mile career, there were quiet times like the night she carried a 67 pound bass around in her trunk. The fish had to be bent a bit to get it into the small confines, but to Wheezer's credit, the trunk didn't fall out. But we might add we had to replace the struts that keep the hatchback in an upright position. Those were around $130 including installation. Do you know how many times one

Wheezer was an all-pro lemon of an automobile complete with roof rack for fish poles.

has to bang one's head before it sinks in your hatchback will not stay up until new struts arrive from whence they've been back ordered? Enough, I'll bet, to make a nifty Advil commercial.

Besides the 67 pounder, there's been other happy moments with Wheezer. For instance, everyone at *The Fisherman* office has become friendly with Mr. Jim Sullivan who owns a Texaco gas station in Mystic, CT. In between fishing excursions, Jim always has a smile for his customers, like the time Gloria, our office manager, called to ask him to send his son with their wrecker over to our office since Wheezer's battery was kaput and it wouldn't start. This was before Wheezer wouldn't start because the timing chain disinvested itself. After paying for the new battery, Jim had a warm word and friendly New England manner as he usually does.

Besides developing an acquaintance with Jim, Wheezer heightened my appreciation of quiet. Once one exits Wheezer's confines one enjoys the luxury of life without pinging. Wheezer, despite the best high test gas money can buy, pings up hill and down dale as she has since the fourth month of our relationship. Other visits to the dealer (besides those for hatchback struts, air conditioner, etc.), produced some temporary quiet, but always the pinging regrouped to rise from the ashes of my check book. Some striper fishermen who wanted to move about unnoticed would never like Wheezer since it's hard to make a quiet entrance when Wheezer's pinging is up to snuff.

I've never tallied how much Wheezer cost in repairs and higher fuel costs, though I can still hear the salesman at the dealership telling me I could use regular no lead thus having a nice economical car. With regular unleaded in Wheezer you'll enjoy a symphony without a radio as you make your way to a 4AM meeting to go bass fishing. For the extra price of high test unleaded, you muffle the orchestra a touch, but will not eliminate it.

The next time I visit the dealer (probably after my next fishing trip), I might try a new pair of shocks since the last time I was there the mechanic wrote on the bill Wheezer was in need. He also wrote down he couldn't locate the new chirp Wheezer is developing somewhere in the front end. The chirp, of course, is different from the ping. If we do a follow-up on this story, we'll let you know outside what fishing location Wheezer broke down this time and what the repair costs were.

We could go on with Wheezer, but you get the idea. If you notice a white, two-door compact sitting out in a deserted field some place near a good fishing spot in Connecticut, Rhode Island or Massachusetts you'll know I broke down and bought a new shotgun. The cost of the new gun was cheap compared with life with Wheezer and it'll feel so good shooting holes in the 'ole son of a gun.

Editor's Update: Prior to press we just heard from the dealer regarding Wheezer's third attempt to have the A/C fixed. Seems there was a short in the wire which they could NOT locate, so they very politely asked me if I could bring the car back another day to have them follow this up. We're not worried; we're very confident the air conditioner will be running perfectly about the time the bass run hits its stride, somewhere on or about November 1st.

Perry the Tackle Man

It had not been a good day for Perry, and it was going to drop off more in just a bit. Perry was standing semi-tall behind his counter, much like you'd find him seven days a week through the fishing season. More than likely he'd have a phone to his ear just as he did that day. Part of him was on the conversation; the other scanned the shop now filling with people.

One of the people started talking while Perry was still on the phone—a sure sign of impatience. The phone party, though, wasn't about to let go of Perry's ear. Over in the background, two employees worked on rod winding: one on a high speed winder; the other by hand. Judging from the rods propped up between the two it was going to be a l-o-n-g time before any dent was made in that wall of fiberglass.

Perry's air conditioner wasn't feeling well at all. The poor machine tried but just couldn't make the mark. Sweat came down Perry's young forehead, a forehead most expected to show signs of grey very soon. Beyond the people standing around the counter (oops, somebody else just came in) were a couple of fishermen sitting on fighting chairs without pedestal bases. The chairs were flush on the floor since Perry had sold the bases. That didn't stop them from sitting and drinking large amounts of free coffee. Every once in awhile one of the sitters would buy something.

But, let's get back to Perry on that summer day. Right in between the phone on one side and impatience on the other, comes Perry's fine wife and ace son, young Tile. Tile was out with Mom and is now the proud owner of a 007-type water pistol filled to the rim. Perry smiled when he saw number one son; maybe, he thought to himself, I'm doing all this for him. Before he can say anything, though, Tile raised the gun and squirted right between the eyes of poor Perry. As the water ran down Perry's nose, people cried when they couldn't laugh any harder. This is a story of the downs, further downs, and extreme lows of a young man who owns a tackle shop.

Perry is a real person, just you watch on "That's Incredible." He runs a small shop with a "little less" space than Sears Roebuck in size. In merchandise and people I sometimes wonder, especially if you were to visit there during a rainy Sunday in January. The hot stove league catches more marlin and tuna there than any place on the globe. Someone once said Perry needs a front-end loader to clear the floor by the time everyone leaves to go watch the afternoon football game. And, every once in awhile, someone does buy something.

Believe this or not, Perry is not on tranquilizers. He takes most things in stride and always seems to be one up on customers looking for tomorrow's tackle yesterday. Occasionally Perry goes so far to say, " Timmy, it's been a bad day." Beyond that, I've never seen him throw anyone through his rear window or raise his voice . I've sniffed the coffee pot a couple times looking for stronger stuff that might be the secret of his calm. Once I thought I had something until I found the pot full of dye for coloring surgical tubing. When's the last time you saw green liquid in a Mr. Coffee? His secret was out, I told myself, until someone cautioned against drinking the brew.

Then there was the time a person came in to buy worms. Perry doesn't sell worms, but that wasn't going to stop that guy. He demanded a dozen. Is this a bait and tackle store or not, he wanted to know? Maybe the guy thought he'd stumbled onto a front for the Cosa Nostra? Perry tried to talk to the guy, to appeal to his intellect and reasoning powers, but that doesn't always work with fishermen. About the third minute of their conversation,

Perry got a brainstorm. He took the guy outside and there for all the world to see was a sign reading Perry's Tackle Company. See, said Perry, it doesn't say anything about bait.

Now Perry figured the guy might buy some hooks or such since he'd politely explained the lack of worms. Would it be fair to think most reasonable people would continue buying after being shown they'd jumped the gun? Well, remember, this guy was a fisherman, who aren't normal people to begin with. Out the front door he went, under the Perry Tackle Company (no worms) sign, probably saying as he went that any store without worms can't be worth much. Some days Perry confronts what some might say are no-win situations. And, every once in awhile, somebody does buy something.

Perry, like a lot of people I admire, advertises in a fine, regional fish wrapper. Once when our unsinkable ad lady visited Perry's place of business she observed another of our advertisers come in under Perry's sign. He picked up a couple three items he needed for an offshore cod trip, then departed without leaving any coin of the realm. Our ad lady stared open-mouthed, then asked Perry about this. Perry just shrugged; it was all in a day's business. Truth be known, Perry and the guy were the best of friends. He would compensate Perry later on when his bill came through. See, I told you—every once in awhile somebody would buy something.

Perry might no sooner be done with ad copy than in walked a wide-eyed surf fanatic just returned from an offshore bass island (aren't all islands offshore?). They're killin' 'em with RedFins, he confided in Perry. At that point, Perry did smile as he had RedFins in black, silver, yellow, blue and white plus a profusion of other colors. No mackerel, asked the guy in disbelief? Another guy took seven fish on the bar last night on a mackerel RedFin with full load, he said; if it's not mackerel I can't use it. Poor Perry, he had no mackerel despite a wall of bass stuff likely to stay the winter.

A side note to the mackerel plug story is Perry might have ordered the hot lures, feeling he finally had all bases covered for the surf nuts. He no sooner got them in, than in comes the editor of a regional fish book. Needlefish, said the man! Needlefish are killin' 'em, nobody is using much in the way of RedFins. Sometimes there's a slight twitch in Perry's left eye that'll develop as business grows.

If bassmen are fussy, some tuna guys get outright demanding and since a lot of them have bucks, they spend big. One day one guy "conversed" with Perry about the whereabouts of his new fighting chair. Perry tried to explain he ordered it six months ago but hadn't heard word one in spite of six phone calls. The man calmly announced if he couldn't get the chair, he'd cancel the $2500 order plus the order for two new custom rods with bent butts and Penn 130s. Sometimes there's a slight twitch in Perry's right eye.

Perry does get days away even during the summer. On one such he elected to run his father's charter boat to the offshore grounds. Aboard were five novice fishermen, one mate and somebody with a movie camera who wanted a flick on high speed trolling. To make a long fight short, Perry did find tuna, but it took over an hour to beat the fish with 50 pound tackle thanks to the inexperienced anglers.

While the fight was going on people called on the radio asking what the hold-up was in landing the unseen fish. And, the fish in the area had stopped biting; so it was either land that one and be a hero or lose it to end up staring blankly at the camera. At one point during the movie you see only Perry's hand gripping the chair on the flybridge, knuckles turning white as the fish refused to give in. At another point you saw Perry looking down into the cockpit, looking for all the world like the best choice for a new aspirin commercial or a 30 second spot for Rolaids.

Perry did beat that tuna thanks to good boat handling; everyone was happy including the camera man. On the three hour ride back home Perry was looking for someone to talk with up there on what can be a lonely flybridge. Not much conversation that day as the camera guy was sound asleep on the floor. Back at the dock people gathered round as the fish weighed in at 108 pounds and members of the group continued their celebration with another round of beers. For some of them, it was their twelfth time around. After everyone took off, Perry went down below to unwind and clean the boat. It was there he found one of his customers had given up his beer, all over the cabin floor and seat.

Now, don't worry about Perry. The next day he was back safe and sound, behind his counter, sure in the knowledge that his dying air conditioner wasn't going to work well that day either.

About the Author

Tim Coleman has fished from different beaches, rockpiles, private and partyboats since he was six. He's made a lot of life's decisions based on the need to be near the water. His interest in angling was interrupted for service in Vietnam and afterwards a B.A. degree in journalism from the University of Rhode Island.

The love of fishing led him to his present job as managing editor of *The New England Fisherman*. Besides his work for *The Fisherman* he's also a free-lance writer and accomplished photographer. His credits include *Outdoor Life, Long Island Fisherman, Salt Water Sportsman, New Jersey Fisherman, Garcia Fishing Annual, Pennsylvania Angler, Mercury Marine's Outdoors, Florida Fishing News*.